PRAISE FOR
WHY TOOTHPASTE MATTERS

"What do you do when you wake up one day and realize that your marriage isn't what you thought it'd be? *Why Toothpaste Matters* addresses that very situation. With humor and authenticity, Kevin and Katie offer practical advice for couples on how to best communicate their expectations to one another."

— Dr. Danny Akin

President, Southeastern Baptist Theological Seminary

Author of *God on Sex: The Creator's Ideas about Love, Intimacy, and Marriage*

"If your marriage is perfect, you have no problems and you never argue, then you probably don't need this book. For the rest of us, *Why Toothpaste Matters* is a wonderful resource. Kevin and Katie Mills have communicated insightful truths about marriage in an easily digestible format."

— Dr. Robert Smith, Jr.

Charles T. Carter Baptist Chair of Divinity

Beeson Divinity School at Samford University

Author of *The Oasis of God: From Mourning to Morning: Biblical Insights from Psalms 42 and 43*

"Whether you find yourself deeply in love right now or on the verge of calling it quits, you will resonate with and find Kevin and Katie's words very relatable. This book is honest, funny, and helpful. The Kevin and Katie you get in this book are the same two people you get having dinner with them in their home. The people behind the message are as real as the message itself. I have no doubt that their journey, and the lessons they have learned from it, will bless yours."

— Dr. Joshua Straub

President / Cofounder, *Famous at Home*

Author of *Safe House* & *What Am I Feeling?*

WHY TOOTHPASTE MATTERS

TEN TRUTHS AND SIX WEEKS TO A BETTER MARRIAGE

Kevin and Katie Mills

Foreword by
Thom Rainer

ISBN: 978-1651788882

CONTENTS

Part 2

Reboot: Six Weeks to a Better Marriage

FOREWORD

It was a simple question the young man asked me, but a complex response was necessary. "Thom," he began, "you and Nellie Jo have been married over 40 years. How have you had such a successful marriage?"

I think my first response was a smile. I do adore my wife, and I thank God for her. But I don't always think of our marriage as "successful." Sometimes, the better word is "surviving" or "persevering."

You see, our marriage has not always been easy. After more than 40 years, I can assure you we have experienced times of challenge and even heartache. In the final analysis, though, my wife and I have been committed to our marriage. We have been determined to stay together. I guess God has honored our tenacity.

WHY TOOTHPASTE MATTERS

I wish we had been given a book like *Why Toothpaste Matters* before we were married. At the very least, I wish we had the book after one year of marriage. Nellie Jo and I never received pre-marital counseling. Our parents never gave us any counsel or guidance. We were two kids who had no idea what we were doing.

What I love about *Why Toothpaste Matters* by Kevin and Katie Mills is both its honesty and its practicality. It is that type of book that you read and say, "I get it. This perspective really helps. This couple really understands me."

Yeah, what a difference this book would have made if I had it four decades ago.

But you have it now.

You are fortunate. You are blessed.

I don't think it's an overstatement to say the book can be transformational. The principles and practices can transform your marriage; it will thus transform your life.

There are at least two ways to savor the content of this book. First, read it alone. Take the ten truths and begin to apply them to your marriage. Seek to serve the Lord by serving your spouse. See what God can do in your life and the life of your spouse.

Second, study the book with a group. It is designed for a nice and compact six-week study. Interact with other couples. Ask questions. Make commitments. See your marriage grow healthier.

Thank you, Kevin and Katie Mills. You have provided us a gift for our marriages. *Why Toothpaste Matters* is a humorous title, but it has a profound message.

Simply stated, this book can make a huge difference in your marriage. I wish I had it over 40 years ago.

But you, the reader, have it now.

Enjoy the blessings the book will give you . . . and your marriage.

Thom Rainer

CEO and Founder of Church Answers

Author of *Anatomy of a Revived Church* and

I Am a Church Member

INTRODUCTION

Virtually every fairy tale romance begins with a hero, an evil villain, and a damsel in distress. The good guy defeats the scoundrel, the knight slays the dragon, the fair maiden is rescued, and the story ends with the usual, anticipated line: "*And they lived happily ever after.*"

If you watch a classic "Rom-Com" movie, the plot will undoubtedly go something like this: boy is attracted to girl, or girl is attracted to boy. Then a series of misunderstandings keeps these two individuals from realizing their love for one another. Or perhaps there are circumstances or individuals obstructing their relationship. For a while, it seems as if this boy and girl (who are obviously meant to be together) will never become a couple. Then, the boy realizes his mistakes, or the girl finally sees what she's been missing, and they work through whatever has kept them apart. The movie ends with this couple kissing as the music swells and the credits roll. End of movie, end of story, everyone is happy, forever and always.

Or scroll through your Facebook or Instagram feed, and invariably you will see the highlight reels of your friends' marriages. A picture of a beautiful bouquet of roses with the caption, "My sweet hubby surprised me with these... and it's not my birthday or our anniversary. Just because he loves me!" Or perhaps a picture of snow white sand with an aqua blue ocean in the background, accompanied by a post reading: "Loving our vacay together!" Of course, we are only seeing what others want us to see; not the mundane, or difficult, or downright nasty days of their lives.

Most of us have consciously or subconsciously bought into the lie that romance is just this easy. Meet the right person and you will have your *happily ever after*. Sure, there might be a couple of bumps along the way. A few rough patches that have to be ironed out. However, they can't be *that* serious, right? That is, if you have married the *right* person. If s/he is "the one" then you should never have any *really* bad issues. Right?

If you've been married for any length of time, you understand reality. Over our years together, we have seen the challenges of marriage, both in our own and in talking with friends about their struggles. Couples begin their marriage believing that it will be a forever honeymoon: full of excitement, laughter, great sex, and deep, endless conversations.

Then, reality sets in.

Time goes by, and things begin to change. He becomes less romantic. She's far more emotional than she was when they were just dating. He's kind of a slob. She suddenly gets headaches whenever he mentions sex. Neither seem to be living up to what the other expected. One morning he wakes up and asks himself how he happened to marry the most selfish person in the world. She starts to wonder what life would be like if she'd married her former boyfriend. Their happily ever after Rom-Com starts to look more like a horror film. They feel stuck, with no clue which next steps to take.

If any of this is or has been true in your marriage, please understand how much you are not alone. Every couple has difficult days, weeks, or even seasons of their marriage. The challenges you have faced, are facing, and will face as a couple are normal. If you are currently in a rough place, it *does not mean* you married the wrong person. It *does mean* you happened to marry another human being who is just as broken and flawed as you. And that you two *less-than-perfect* people made the decision to share every aspect of your lives together: you live in the same residence and share the same address. You pay bills together and share the same finances. You socialize with the same friends. You spend holidays with relatives, sharing the same families. You share your physical bodies with one another. If you have children, you share in parenting. Unlike any other relationship you've ever had before, you are operating your life in partnership with your spouse.

WHY TOOTHPASTE MATTERS

Think about your past relationships: If you had siblings growing up, you undoubtedly fought with them. Yet, you only shared the same address and family, not finances and children. Perhaps you've had conflict with a business partner or co-worker. In that relationship, you shared finances, but not family. If you had a previous long-term relationship where you were involved sexually, you likely had conflict. Yet, while you were physically connected, you were not sharing children or finances.

However, in marriage, you are connected in every way. Two people involved at such a deep level shouldn't be surprised at all when they disagree about how they should operate in their shared lives. Her actions affect him. His decisions impact her life. No husband can just say, "Well, it's her life. She needs to live it however she wants." No wife can say, "I really don't care *what* he does." This approach will not work with two lives so intertwined. Therefore, we should expect there to be conflict. Even serious, really intense conflict. The "you're sleeping on the couch" and "I don't want to see your face for a while" kind of fights.

Once again, if this has happened to you, you're not alone. Virtually every couple has experienced these kinds of conflicts, including us. That is why we decided to write this book.

The following chapters are divided into sections. Some are written from Kevin's perspective, and some are written from Katie's. We've tried to be very open about our own struggles and transparent in our feelings. At times, writing these words was emotionally gut-wrenching, and we nearly didn't complete the book. As a couple in ministry, we fear what others will now think of us, knowing that our marriage hasn't always been perfect. Will we be seen as "less than spiritual" by some? Will others believe that Kevin shouldn't be leading a group of Christ-followers if he's having problems in his marriage? Will there be those who now question our relationship, wondering if our marriage is truly healthy enough for us to be in our current ministry?

> *Happily ever after is certainly ideal, but it's just not reality.*

At the end of the day, we felt that we needed to push these questions aside. Sure, there are a few who may judge or look down their noses from their lofty place of a spiritually perfect marriage, but they represent a minuscule percentage of the population. The rest of us understand this truth: when two sinners live together in the same home, share the same bed, bathroom, finances, friends, children, in-laws, calendar, and virtually every other aspect of life, conflict is inevitable. *Happily ever after* is certainly ideal, but it's just not reality.

This is why we have decided to tell our story, as well as offer some practical advice. Our hope is that you will be able to use this book as a way to "reboot" your own marriage. The first section of the book contains ten chapters, each highlighting a truth about marriage. These are designed for you to simply read and reflect on how the chapters apply to your life and marriage. The second section contains six chapters with discussion questions at the end of each chapter. These are intended for you and your spouse to use in the "rebooting" of your marriage. Our recommendation is — after reading the first section of the book — to plan "date nights" for the next six weeks. Pick one night during the week to go to dinner, take a picnic to your favorite park, or put the kids to bed early and have a stay at home date. Then, use the questions in the second section to guide your discussion. Give your spouse permission to be honest. Allow him/her to speak freely. Listen carefully to one another. Ask follow-up questions. Ask questions not included in the chapter. Then spend some time talking through solutions and action steps the two of you can take to overcome any of those issues you are facing in your marriage.

While this book will not fix every current or future problem in your marriage, these discussions will be invaluable for helping you understand the expectations you have of one another and, hopefully, improve communication between you and your spouse.

Our heartfelt hope and prayer is that six weeks from today, your marriage will not simply be surviving, but on the road to thriving.

Kevin and Katie Mills

PART 1

TEN TRUTHS ABOUT MARRIAGE

CHAPTER 1

THE PROBLEM WITH TOOTHPASTE

Marriage Truth #1:
You'll have fights you never could have
imagined while you were dating.

~ KEVIN ~

They sat on the couch in my office, she on one end and he on the other. Her arms were folded over her body as if she were protecting herself from a cold wind on a winter day. He had one leg crossed over the other, both of his hands grasping onto his right knee. His left elbow rested on the leather arm of the couch so that his body tilted as far to the edge as possible. The physical space between this couple conveyed the even greater relational gap that now existed in their lives.

Only eighteen months earlier, this couple sat in my office on the same couch. Then, however, they placed themselves in the middle, both sitting on one leather seat cushion. Their jeans connected at the hips and thighs, and they held hands with fingers interlocked, resting this melded flesh on their knees. Each time he spoke, she'd look up at his face with a combination of adoration and yearning. His broad grin and the gleam in his eyes reflected the desires of his heart. Every word spoken and every nonverbal movement signaled their passionate love for one another.

A few weeks prior to our initial meeting, this couple took an online premarital counseling test. They answered questions related to finances, family, spiritual beliefs, sexual expectations, and several other spheres of life. The results of this test indicated a number of potential issues this young couple would face in their marriage. They were not fully aligned in their beliefs or in their expectations. Their backgrounds were varied enough that I knew there would be conflicts in their future. While every couple brings different ideas of what is "normal" into a marriage, this particular guy and girl would be singing from two very different sheets of music for a period of time. They needed to discuss and work through these differences. My job was to help them consider and explore these areas of potential conflict now, in the relaxed and unemotional environment of premarital counseling. Hopefully, as they revealed to one another their desires and hopes, they would later avoid the heated arguments and passionate disputes when one or both partners failed to live up to the other's expectations.

"Let's talk about finances," I began. "This is a big one. Unless you happen to be ridiculously rich (I knew they weren't), most of the fights you'll have will be over money. You'll argue over major purchases, minor purchases, how much to save, and even how much money you earn. It will be the greatest source of tension in your marriage. According to your test, you guys have very different approaches to money. One of you is a spender, and one is a saver. This is something you need to talk through now; otherwise, you'll find yourselves in some major fights. Okay, the first thing I need to ask you is this: Have you guys created a budget?"

"A what?" the guy asked.

"A family budget. You have an idea of what your expenses will be, and you know what you're going to be making in your jobs. Have you put a budget to paper yet?"

I had difficulty reading her expression, but I understood his perfectly. His smile wasn't really a smile. It was a smirk. "I think we'll be okay without a budget," he said. "We'll just figure it out as we go."

> "Uh, no," he said with a chuckle. "I can't imagine us ever having a serious fight."

"You will?" I asked. "Don't you think you'll end up fighting a lot?"

"Uh, no," he said with a chuckle. "I can't imagine us ever having a serious fight."

"Me neither," she quickly chimed in.

What crazy planet are you two living on? I wanted to ask.

Instead, I said, "What makes you think this?"

"We are *in love*," he responded, emphasizing and elongating the word, *love*. He paused for a moment, then turned his head to his fiancé and spoke to her directly while patting her arm. "Love will carry us through whatever problems we face."

The remainder of the counseling session was a perfunctory exercise. My advice fell on deaf ears. There was no way I would get through to this couple. Remember, they were in *l..o..v..e*.

Eighteen months later, they once again sat on my couch. This time, however, I had two individuals who were more than willing to listen. In counseling, it's what we call a *teachable moment*. When life has taken a particularly bad turn, or someone has hit rock bottom, and the individual is more-than-willing to listen to the wisdom of a parent or another authority figure — that's a teachable moment. This was one of those times. Their marriage was not what they'd expected it to be. The dynamics of their relationship had shifted. They had removed the rose-colored glasses. Reality had set in. Now, they were ready to talk and, *more importantly*, they were ready to listen.

"So tell me the issue," I said.

"Ask her," he grunted. "I thought everything was fine. But, according to her, I can't do *anything* right."

She was nearly in tears, but managed to keep her composure as she tried to explain her feelings. "He doesn't care about me. I'll clean the whole apartment, and he won't say a thing. Worse yet, I'll have the apartment perfectly organized, and he'll just throw his dirty socks on the floor. Or leave his dirty dishes sitting on the coffee table. Or the toothpaste thing. He knows how much it drives me crazy!" She started to sniffle, and it gave me a chance to ask the question her last statement had raised.

"I'm sorry," I said. "What's the toothpaste thing?"

"Oh, she gets all crazy over the toothpaste," he practically shouted. "She can't stand it when I forget to put the top back onto the tube. She always leaves for work before me, and so most mornings I will have ESPN on the television in the bedroom while I'm getting ready. Sometimes I'll get distracted when I hear some update or story about a team, and I'll put the toothpaste onto my brush and forget to put the top back onto the tube. I'll finish getting ready, head out the door, and, well, *God-forbid*, I left the top sitting there on the counter and forgot to put it back onto the tube. She gets home from work and sees the topless toothpaste. Then I come home and we have to have a sit-down, full-scale conference about how awful I've been and how I never take her feelings into account. Right when I walk through the door, I'm hit with a crying wife who calls me the devil over *toothpaste*. Is it *really* that big of a deal?"

"It's gross," she said with water-filled eyes. "And it's not just about the toothpaste. It's about the fact that *you know* how much it bothers me, yet you refuse to do anything about it. It's like my feelings don't matter to you at all!"

> *"A good, healthy marriage requires more than romantic feelings."*

"You see, Pastor. You see how dramatic she is! She can't just let something go. Every little thing gets blown up into this major issue where I don't care about her feelings. This is why we're fighting all the time!"

"You're fighting all the time?" I asked. "But that can't be. I thought you two were in l..o..v..e."

I didn't really say that. It was tempting, but this was no moment for sarcasm. They were struggling and needed my help. The toothpaste was the presenting problem, but there were deep emotions and baggage behind that topless tube. We spent the next hour talking about toothpaste and a number of other topics.

This couple, who eighteen months earlier couldn't have imagined themselves fighting in this way, now faced a reality that exists in every marriage: just being *in love* isn't enough. A good, healthy marriage requires more than romantic feelings. A marriage that lasts must be built on more than just a foundation of passion. While the fireworks and sentimental emotions are wonderful and necessary, they are not nearly enough and can only carry the marriage so far. When they fade away, the couple will find themselves sitting on a couch in front of a counselor or pastor, yelling about toothpaste.

Your marriage is like a garden. You must be intentional about tending this garden. At times, you'll need to water, or prune the plants, or pull weeds, or add a little fertilizer. If you fail to do these things, your marriage will continue to grow for a little while, but eventually the lack of attention will begin to show. The neglect will manifest itself in lots of ways: fights, isolation, irritation, coldness...the list goes on and on.

Conversely, making the decision to show your marriage the attention it needs — to care for this garden — will bring great health and happiness to your relationship.

Working through this book together is the act of you and your spouse tending to the garden. As you both read through the chapters and discuss these marriage truths, you're nourishing your marriage. Going through the questions will help protect your relationship from disease and infestation. Even if it's hard work now, you'll enjoy a great harvest later.

If you're almost or newly married, you probably think all of this work is unnecessary. You may have trouble imagining your relationship ever feeling like *work*. You've married someone who has brought such great joy and happiness to your life, so you just can't understand why couples ever have serious fights. You are in *l..o..v..e* and believe that fighting is reserved for those couples without a love as strong as yours.

If this is your mindset, please be sure to read the next chapter.

CHAPTER 2

THE LOVE LIE

Marriage Truth #2:
Your spouse isn't designed to fill
the deepest needs of your heart.

~ KEVIN ~

I came of age in the 1980's and 90's, a time when love itself became an altar where my generation happily went to worship. Romantic movies and songs flooded our lives, all proclaiming this truth: *If you want salvation, then look for it in the perfect relationship.* Sacrifice everything to get this relationship. Abandon all for this relationship. In the end, it's only love that matters.

Think I'm exaggerating? Consider the classic scene from the 1989 film, *Say Anything*, where John Cusack stands outside the second-story window of the girl he loves with a boombox raised high above his head. In a thoroughly 80's way of serenading a romantic interest, Cusack plays Peter Gabriel's *In Your Eyes*, proclaiming to this girl: "In your eyes, I am complete... I see the doorway to a thousand churches... I want to be that complete... to touch the light, the heat I see in your eyes."[1]

Great movie. Excellent song. Bad message.

Or consider the words Tom Cruise declares to Renee Zellweger in the 1996 movie, *Jerry Maguire*. The climactic moment of the movie comes when he professes his willingness to commit everything to her because, "You complete me." Without her, he realizes, he isn't all he's able or supposed to be. Only in this relationship will he find true fulfillment in life.

Great movie. Superb acting. Bad message.

What about the 1990 blockbuster *Pretty Woman*? All the moral issues of hiring a prostitute and then dating this woman are overcome by their love for one another. Her past, his past, their baggage, their current hangups... all of these are instantaneously erased and made irrelevant when Richard Gere shows up outside of her balcony, his head and torso sticking out the sunroof of his limousine, holding a dozen roses. His willingness to commit his all to her becomes their salvation.

Great movie. Pretty actress. Bad message.

Or consider virtually every song by Peter Cetera, both when he was the lead singer for *Chicago* and when he embarked upon his solo career:

- *You're the meaning in my life, you're the inspiration. You bring feeling to my life, you're the inspiration.*[2]
- *I am a man who will fight for your honor, I'll be the hero you're dreaming of. We'll live forever, knowing together that we did it all for the glory of love.*[3]
- *After all that we've been through, I will make it up to you, I promise to. And after all that's been said and done, you're just the part of me I can't let go.*[4]

Meaning and eternal life are all found in this romantic relationship. They will live forever in the glory of love. She's become so much a part of him that he can't let her go.

Great songs. Terrific crooner. Bad message.

There are thousands of other songs just like these, all proclaiming the same truth. The right person will bring to our lives "meaning," "inspiration," and "feeling." When we are down, this person will rescue us and cause us to cry out, "No one needs you more than I. *need. you.*"

Each song seems to place a spotlight on two people whose passion for one another is so strong, whose hearts are so perfectly in-tune, and whose feelings for one another are so absolutely overwhelming that nothing can ever tear them apart.

> **We** long for what's been called the "super relationship."

WHY TOOTHPASTE MATTERS

This message of our culture has caused us to believe the lie that being with the right person will solve all of our problems. We long for what's been called the "*super relationship*." We want to fall in love with someone who will meet our deepest needs, provide us inspiration, be our soul mate, and supply perfect intimacy. We believe that the *right* person, once found, will fill all the empty places of our lives and give us the peace we've always longed for.

Kind of makes that person sound like God, doesn't it?

This belief places an expectation on another person that is impossible for any individual to fulfill. No human relationship can provide that for you. No matter how wonderful he or she is, they can never fully or always be your inspiration, provide you with meaning, and bring all the perfect feelings to your life. Yet, our culture has programmed our minds and hearts to believe this lie. We subconsciously place these expectations on our spouse. You begin to believe lies such as:

- The deepest longings of my heart should be fulfilled by my soulmate.
- Nothing else matters as long as my heart tells me it's true.
- As long as we are in love, we will never have any serious fights.
- My purpose and happiness are found completely in this other person.
- If I'm not happy, I must've married the wrong person.

These beliefs will cause tremendous issues in your

relationship. What happens when the day comes that he's not very inspiring, or she's not providing much meaning, and both of you are full of feelings, but not the kind in one of Peter Cetera's songs? What do you do when the emotions seem to match more with the song by The J. Geils Band, *Love Stinks*? You will likely become frustrated and angry, wondering why your fairytale romance has suddenly gone terribly wrong.

> *In Song of Solomon, love is celebrated as a gift from God, not a substitute for God.*

"Hold on just a minute," you might say. "Aren't we supposed to have these strong emotions and passion for the person we've married? Shouldn't we have the fireworks and butterflies and all the mushy feelings? Even the Bible describes romance as a good thing. Isn't Song of Solomon all about a guy's intense love for a girl, his pursuit of her, and her desire for him?"

Absolutely. And all of those thoughts and feelings are celebrated. The difference is this: in Song of Solomon, love is celebrated as a gift *from* God, not a substitute *for* God. God loves giving good gifts to us, and romance, marriage, and sex are among his best gifts. It excites God to see his creation *enjoying* and *celebrating* these things, but not *elevating* these gifts above him.

Which is exactly what Gen Xers did. And Gen Y's. And now the Millennials are doing the same thing. Every generation, in its own way, seeks to find in others what is only meant to be found in God.

And it's causing a lot of chaos and heartache. Each year,

thousands of couples are standing before a pastor, a judge, or the friend who managed to secure a quick internet ordination. In front of their families and friends, they make a lifetime commitment to another person. Yet, they do so because they've bought into this lie. She believes he will always make her feel a certain way. He makes promises believing that she will perfectly fill a void in his life. They both are expecting the other to be the anchor in this super relationship.

When this false foundation begins to crumble... when he's no longer the meaning in her life... when she's no longer his inspiration.. when neither are bringing much feeling into the life of their spouse... that's when the marriage begins to implode. Expectations aren't met, even though they were impossible to meet in the first place. He begins to wonder if he made a mistake in marrying too soon. She tries to figure out ways to "fix" this guy she married. Both are frustrated, and they can't understand why the reality of their marriage is so different from what they imagined it would be.

Somehow we've bought into the lie that marrying the right guy or girl will make our lives virtually perfect. This lie creates impossible expectations, and unmet expectations will cause a lot of destruction.

Which is exactly what Katie writes about in the next chapter.

CHAPTER 3

THE FESTIVUS FIGHT

*Marriage Truth #3: Unmet expectations
will cause most of your arguments.*

~ KATIE ~

It's funny that Kevin wrote about the movie, *Pretty Woman*. I love that movie. During my college years, I owned a television with a built-in VCR (it was old school even back then) and I had that movie on a VHS tape. There were so many times I would have it playing in the background as I put on my make-up or decided which outfit I would wear to dinner with friends. I love the way this movie makes me feel. What began as just a physical relationship turns out to be a wonderful romance. She filled a void in his life he didn't even know he had. He was willing to kill a lucrative business deal just to make her happy. They end the movie riding off into the sunset together, happily ever after.

Yeah, I'm pretty sure I bought into the lie.

It's just so easy to believe. If I meet the right guy, then I'll truly be happy. He'll just know when I've had a bad day and will give me the emotional support I need. He'll be able to read my mind. He'll know exactly what I need, when I need it. He will forever and always be my happily ever after. I walked down the aisle of a church cradling this belief in my arms.

Little did I know that my fairy tale bubble would soon burst wide open.

We'd been married about three months. Kevin was working full time on staff at the church we attended. I was teaching at an elementary school in Charlotte, North Carolina, the city where we met and married. His job allowed him to take most Fridays off since he worked all day on Sunday. During those first several weeks of our marriage, when I arrived home at five or six o'clock on a Friday, the house had been cleaned and plans had been made. We were going to dinner or he'd rented a DVD for us to watch or we were hanging out with some friends. My only job was to go along with whatever he had us doing together.

Then it happened. It was a Friday afternoon in September of 2005. I found myself getting excited during the nearly half hour commute I had from the school to our house. It'd been a particularly rough week and an especially rough day. My twenty-seven second graders were enthusiastic about the weekend, but not really about schoolwork. I'd struggled all day. What held me back from screaming at a classroom full of seven and eight year olds was my anticipation about that Friday evening. I'd get to relax, hang out with my husband, and he'd handle everything.

I walked in the door of our home and saw him sitting on our couch with his feet propped up on the ottoman. He was wearing khakis and a dress shirt. I'd forgotten — he had to work that Friday. All day. I remember thinking on the drive home from school, "It's weird that he's not called or texted me to let me know what we are doing tonight. He normally gives me a heads up, especially if he thinks it's something I might not want to do. Maybe he's got a big surprise for me tonight. I can't wait!"

Then I walked in the door. There he was, his shirt untucked, shoes off, and leaning back against the armrest of our couch. He had one hand across his chest, the television remote in the other, and was watching a rerun of *Seinfeld*. I'm not sure he even heard me come into the house. Or he did, but he seemed to be more interested in this ridiculous show than in me.

"Hey," I said, trying to get him to look my way. "Watcha doing?"

> **He** *seemed to be more interested in this ridiculous show than in me.*

"Nothing," he said, not even glancing at me. I was hoping he'd get up from his nearly horizontal position, walk over to me, give me a hug and kiss, and then tell me about the wonderful plans we had for the evening.

"Ummm, okay. So, what are you thinking about us doing tonight?"

"I have no idea. I walked in ten minutes before you did. I was the only pastor in the office and worked like a one-armed wall-paper hanger all day long. I just haven't thought about it."

The whole time he was talking, he never took his eyes off the television. Some old man was telling this guy with crazy hair all about a holiday he'd invented. "At the Festivus dinner, you gather your family around," the older man said, "and tell them all the ways they have disappointed you over the past year!"

"Is there a tree?" Crazy Hair asked.

"No, instead there's a pole. Requires no decoration." Then he said something about tinsel being distracting and going to get a pole out of his basement. Such an idiotic show. Just a bunch of guys talking about nothing. And the one token girl also talking about nothing. Yet, their absurd discussions about a fictional winter holiday had completely captured my husband's attention. Moreover, I knew he'd seen this episode before. Likely *many times* before, because I can remember him talking about this Festivus holiday and quoting lines I was now hearing in our den. He eas-ily could've stopped watching this stupid show for one minute, worked himself up out of his slumber, walked over to me, hugged me, and said something like, "Let's come up with something fun for tonight. What do you feel like doing?" Or anything like that. Instead, he was laser-focused on Jerry and George, Crazy Hair and the old man, and not at all on me. I just wanted his attention for one minute, and to know that my *husband-of-less-than-three-months* and I would be doing something together that evening. Going to a movie. Grabbing dinner at one of our favorite places. Renting a movie. Anything. Well, anything except vegging on the couch watching reruns of 90's sitcoms.

All of these thoughts hit me really hard. I walked the five or so steps from our den into the kitchen (our first house was rather small). I flung my purse onto our breakfast table and fell into one of the chairs. I put my elbows on the table, rested my face in my hands, and began to cry. Looking back, I realize that it was a big overreaction to the circumstances, but it was genuinely how I felt. I wanted his attention, and I wasn't getting it.

> ❝ *I wanted his attention,*
> *and I wasn't getting it.* ❞

A minute or so later I heard a commercial blaring from the television set. This evidently released my husband from his hypnotic trance, and he somehow managed to pry himself off the couch. He walked over to me and saw me sitting at our table, sobbing. "What in the world happened?" he practically shouted. Being new at the whole marriage thing, he wasn't yet accustomed to my crying. Tears generally sent him into overdrive, believing that something was seriously wrong. It would be a few years before he would eventually figure out how quickly and easily female tears can be produced. A Hallmark movie; missing a big sale; PMS; a dismissive text from a friend; they can all be a catalyst for turning on the waterworks.

"Are you hurt?" he continued. "What's wrong?"

"I expected you would've had something planned for us," I said through my sobs.

"You what?"

"I just didn't expect to spend this evening doing nothing. Or watching a show about nothing. I expected to come home and you'd have something planned for us to do."

He stood there, looking at me with a mixture of confusion and frustration. After a few seconds, with a tone of complete exasperation, he said, "Well, I just expected to arrive home and you'd be wearing nothing but Saran Wrap, but, you know, here we are."

Not funny, I thought. Not funny one bit. "What are we going to do tonight?" I said, hoping he'd at least *attempt* to salvage this evening.

"I don't know. Let me know when you have it planned. I'm going to change clothes." Then he marched off to our bedroom.

I'm pretty sure it was the first really serious fight we had as a married couple.

There is this huge truth that Kevin and I have learned in our marriage. It's true for us, and I bet it's true in your marriage as well. The truth is this: *Expectations are everything.* It's not nearly as much about what actually happens or doesn't happen, what he actually says or doesn't say, or what actual plans are or are not made. What matters is what I expect to happen, or what I expect him to say, or what plans I expect him to make. Our biggest fights happen when I expect one thing, but reality is something completely different. That's when I'm left hurt and angry, sitting at the kitchen table crying. Or when he expects one thing, but it doesn't happen. Then he marches off to the bedroom and our entire evening falls apart.

Unmet expectations are relationship killers. When we expect our spouse to act one way, *and they don't*, that's when things go south. That's when our feelings are hurt and the fight begins. Not necessarily because what they did or didn't do was so bad or that big of a deal. It's just not what we *expected*. And that unmet expectation causes tension in the marriage.

This is why *communication* is the key to any healthy marriage. Let's go back to the earlier scenario. Imagine if that morning, before I'd left the house, I'd simply said, "You know what? I'm super excited about whatever we are doing tonight." Kevin would've responded, "Hey, remember that I'm working in the office all day and won't be home until six or so. I'll try and stop to rent a movie on the way home. How does that sound?"

> *Unmet expectations are relationship killers.*

Or imagine I'd called him during my very brief lunch break and talked through our after-work plans.

Or, on my way home, instead of calling that friend I'd been

meaning to call back for three days, I'd called Kevin and asked, "Hey, do you have any plans for tonight?"

Any number of scenarios would have led to a much different outcome that evening; one that wouldn't have ended with me sitting at our table crying and him storming off to the bedroom. It's not that the situation would've been any different. He most likely would've still been lying horizontally on the couch, remote in hand, trying to recover from his busy day. It just wouldn't have surprised me to walk into the house and hear Crazy Hair's voice blasting from our television. My *expectations* for the evening would've been in line with reality. And *that* would've changed everything.

The exercises at the end of this book are designed to help you and your spouse communicate expectations on lots of areas of life — from the mundane to the magnificent. As you talk through your hopes, dreams, and desires, reasonable and realistic expectations will form. And as unmet expectations decrease, so will your fights.

CHAPTER 4

I MARRIED FOR BETTER, BUT (S)HE GOT WORSE!

Marriage Truth #4:
Just because you fight doesn't mean
you married the wrong person.

~ KEVIN ~

As a pastor, I have performed dozens of weddings during my years in ministry. I've officiated some that were BIG ceremonies, and others that were very small affairs with just a handful of individuals present. I've officiated weddings of couples who were in their twenties and couples who were in their fifties.

In every wedding, I will say these words to the bride and the groom, and have them repeat after me: "I _____, *take you* _____, *to be my wedded wife/husband; to have and to hold; from this day forward; for better or for worse; for richer or poorer; in sickness and in health; to love and to cherish; till death do us part.*"

Each time, I've asked both the groom and the bride to say those vows. To the best of my knowledge, every couple genuinely meant what they said. The vows were more than just words; they represented the true, honest expressions of their hearts.

And yet, for so many couples, after a few months, or a few years, or maybe a decade or two, they would say something like this: "Sure, I said for better and for worse, but I had no idea just how *much worse* it could actually get. I know what I said, and I meant what I said, but this, *this* is not at all how I thought it would be."

I've never known a couple who married expecting their marriage to fail. Maybe there are some in existence, but I've not met this couple. I've not met a groom who has said, "Yeah, we are getting married in June, but I'm pretty sure we'll divorce in a year or two. So I'm keeping my *eharmony.com* profile active, you know, just in case." I've not met a bride who has planned the wedding, purchased a dress, selected bridesmaids' dresses, worked on the one thousand details of the ceremony, but through it all believed it would only be a temporary marriage.

Every husband and wife I've known married with the full expectation that they would be able to go the distance. He popped the question because he believed that their marriage would last a lifetime. She walked down the aisle imagining that they would grow old together. They each said, "Till death do us part," and *sincerely...genuinely... wholeheartedly...* meant the words they spoke.

Yet, we all know the statistics. Half of those marriages end in divorce. Fifty percent do not go the distance. One out of every two couples do not grow old together. For better becomes so much worse that their mindset changes. What once was believed to be a forever relationship becomes intolerable and impossible. He, she, or both come to the conclusion that life would become better if they were no longer together. So, they hire attorneys, file with the courts, sign the paperwork, move into separate residences, and begin the process of living life apart from the other person. The images of growing old together fade away. Their future hopes, dreams, and plans as a couple are extinguished. They divorce and move on with their lives.

> *I've never known a couple who married expecting their marriage to fail.*

Why is this the case? A common belief is that some couples (the ones who stay together) have successfully found "the one." They argue that we are all destined to marry a specific person, much like Cinderella and Prince Charming being guided by the fairy godmother into one another's arms. When we find that individual, then we will truly live, "happily ever after." The right person will bring the right feelings, and this is what will make the relationship work well.

WHY TOOTHPASTE MATTERS

This is certainly possible for a period of time. A new romance with all of the excitement and strong passions for one another will fuel the relationship for a while. The fairy tale feelings will enable each partner to look past the flaws of the other and to work exceedingly hard at ensuring the success of the relationship.

When Katie and I first started dating, we went to dinner late one evening and then drove back to her apartment. We sat in my car talking for a couple of hours, then I walked her inside her apartment. It was after midnight, and I remember thinking that I needed to go home because I had a 7 AM breakfast meeting with some coworkers the next day. Well, technically, it was that same day... in less than seven hours. I would have to drive home, sleep, shower, dress, and get to my breakfast meeting all in, well, now, six hours and forty-five minutes.

At this point in her life, Katie taught second grade at an elementary school. I also knew she would need to be in her classroom at 7:30 AM the next... I mean, *that* day. It was late and I needed to leave. I was just about to say, "I need to go, you've got to work and I've got this breakfast meeting," when Katie said, "I'm thirsty." She walked into her kitchen and opened a cabinet door to get a glass. "Do you want something to drink?"

I don't remember being the least bit thirsty, but said something like, "Sure, I'll take a cafe latte."

"How about ice water?"

"Yeah, that will do."

She walked out of the kitchen with two glasses, and we made

our way over to the couch in her den and sat down. We stayed there, holding hands and talking, for the next four hours. I arrived home a little after four o'clock in the morning, slept for a couple of hours, then went to my early breakfast meeting. I was exhausted, but all smiles. The newness of the relationship and the passion I felt made it seem effortless. Staying up all night wasn't a big deal. I would've walked barefoot over hot burning coals if that were the only way to be with her.

Now, nearly a decade and a half later, if she wants to have a conversation past 9 PM, my eyelids suddenly become unbearably heavy. Even a cafe latte isn't enough to keep me talking and holding hands with her until four o'clock in the morning.

Our story certainly isn't unique. Every couple I know goes through this "falling in love" stage. They talk on the phone for hours. She only sees his positive traits. She can do no wrong in his eyes. They are Prince Charming and Cinderella at the ball, with emotional jet fuel propelling their relationship.

Then, after a month, or six months, or a year, reality sets in. Prince Charming loses some of his charm. Or his hair. The six-pack he had on their wedding day begins to look more like a barrel. He doesn't listen like he did when they were dating. Golf with his buddies takes priority over the couples shower she wants them to attend.

Similarly, Cinderella starts to change. Her insecurities begin to surface. She doesn't offer the nightly shoulder rubs like she did when they were engaged. She gains a little weight. The sexy negligees she once wore to bed are traded in for ragged sweatpants.

Additionally, all the positive traits that were once so magnified begin to become overshadowed by previously ignored negative traits. When they dated, he thought her desire to shop and have the latest clothes showed off her classy sense of style. Now he's frustrated every month looking at their credit card bill. She thought he was so cool when he was around his guy friends. Now she thinks they are all just a bunch of little boys who can't seem to grow up.

Then you add in money problems and family issues and work schedules and, well, that toothpaste deal. Why can't he seem to get that top back on the tube of toothpaste?

When reality replaces romance, a false belief often surfaces: I *married the wrong person*. If she really was THE one, my romantic feelings wouldn't have faded. If he really was my Prince Charming, then life would still be like a fairy tale. I must have missed it. I must have married the wrong person. What should I do now?

Before I go any further, let's examine the fallacy of this belief. If it were true — that we all have "the one" we are supposed to marry — then what happens if just one couple misses their "one" destined for them? If Julie is supposed to marry John, but John marries Ashley, then what does Julie do? She marries Cory, whose "one" was Madeline. And since Madeline didn't marry Cory, who was her "one," she marries David instead. David's "one" was Kristen, but he missed it by marrying Madeline, so now Kristen is in a real pickle. So she marries...

You see how if just one couple gets it wrong, the whole system breaks down?

This notion that we all have one person we are destined to

marry only works if every single person gets it right every time. Therefore, if you believe this to be true, then whoever you marry is, in fact, your "one." Philosophically and theologically speaking, he's your Prince Charming. She's your Cinderella. You've married the right person.

> **Who you marry isn't nearly as important as how you work at your marriage.**

More practically, however, is another fact we need to remember when the romance begins to fade. Virtually every marriage will work if the couple is willing to work at it. No marriage will work if the couple isn't willing to work at it. *Who you marry* isn't nearly as important as *how you work at your marriage.* Did you get that last sentence? As you consider the condition of your marriage, the qualities of your spouse are low on the list of contributing factors. The effort s(he) and you are putting into your marriage relationship are vastly more important.

Again, reading and going through the exercises in the next section of this book are great steps. Whether your marriage is currently in a healthy place and this is merely a check-up, or you feel like your marriage is in the crash-and-burn stage, working through these questions together will do so much to breathe life into your relationship.

And for you and "the one" you married, your best days are ahead.

CHAPTER 5

THE POWER STRUGGLE

Marriage Truth #5:
You and your spouse are both selfish.

~ KEVIN ~

Early in the book of Genesis, we read about the first couple rebelling against God. When they do, sin and evil enter the world. Labor pain, disease, sunburns, cuts, bruises, emotional pain, tornadoes, famines... God's perfect paradise was shattered, and we now live in a world where brokenness is all around us.

Obviously, the marriage relationship was greatly affected by this rebellion. After their decision to disobey his instructions, God spoke to Eve and gave her a heads up about what was coming: "To the woman he said...Your desire will be for your husband, and he will rule over you" (Genesis 3:16b, NIV). The New Living Translation reads, "You will desire to control your husband, but he will rule over you."

Here was the warning God gave to Eve: there would exist a power struggle within their marriage. God knew this introduction of sin into our world would cause us all to become selfish, and that this selfishness would manifest itself the most in a marriage relationship. This would create a constant tension between husbands and wives over who would get their way.

The power struggle in marriage is interesting. The classic view is that God called the husband to be the head of the household, and the wife is to be under the husband's authority. While God established the household to operate in this manner, God also recognized that it wouldn't be this simple. Or, rather, this easy. The husband will rule over the wife, but she won't like it. At all. In fact, she'll subtly and sometimes not-so-subtly try to flip this structure so that, in reality, she has the power. Even in homes where both husband and wife hold to this traditional view of marriage, there exists a tension.

Why is this so? Because we are all born as selfish individuals. I'm selfish, my wife is selfish, you and your spouse are selfish. Even if you are now a follower of Christ and have been forgiven completely of every sin and selfish act, you will still, at times, fall into the clutches of sin. Your natural desire to meet your own needs first will be on full display in your marriage.

In premarital counseling, I warn every couple that marriage

is unlike any other relationship in life. As mentioned in the introduction of the book, marriage is wholly unique. In every other relationship you have in life, you have a bond or maybe even several bonds. You can have a roommate where you share the bond of a same address. You can have a business partner, and share the same finances. You can have a girlfriend or boyfriend and have the bond of a sexual relationship.

But in marriage, you share every one of those bonds: same address, same finances, same bed, and most often, the same children. Many times you share the same friends. Virtually every relationship bond that is possible, you share with this individual. The Bible refers to marriage as "becoming one" for good reason. You are connected on every level.

Being this intertwined means you'll have conflict. Even in the healthiest of marriages there will be fights and quarrels and times when you honestly believe you are sleeping with the enemy. It is impossible to erase all the effects of "The Fall" in our lives. If you've ever made a statement like, "There's no one else who gets me as mad as my spouse," then you are not alone. So much of life overlaps with this other individual. Therefore, conflict is inevitable.

> *The Bible refers to marriage as "becoming one" for good reason. You are connected on every level.*

Additionally, you see the real, unfiltered, morning breath, naked versions of one another. The people at your office and your network of friends see the you after you've showered, brushed your teeth, and put on clothes and makeup. They see a facade. Your spouse sees the real you. Therefore, you will at times go head to head with this person who gets the unfiltered you. You want your way, they want their way, and the power struggle continues.

This is why working at your marriage is both critically important and incredibly challenging. The marriage curse of "I want my way" described in Genesis will completely destroy your marriage if you're not careful to both *recognize* and *deal* with the problem. You and your spouse have to shift your perspectives. Instead of, "I'm going to do whatever I can to get my way in this marriage," the right question to ask is, "What can I do to help my spouse be a better / healthier / happier person?" When *that* becomes your goal, you get a better spouse, and you get a healthier marriage, and you get a happier you.

We have four children. As of this writing, they are 10, 9, 4, and 3. Which means that (unless all of them happen to be asleep) our house is pretty chaotic. I have a home office I rarely use because, well, it's just too loud and lively around our house.

Katie does a tremendous job of managing the business of our home. She coordinates schedules and groceries and washing clothes and the thousand other daily tasks required to keep *www.mills.com* operating. But, sometimes, it starts to get to her, and she needs a break. She needs me to step in and become "her" so she can go to dinner with friends or just hide out in our bedroom for a little while.

Other times, she'll reach a more serious breaking point. She'll say to me, "Look, I love these kids with all my heart, but one of them is about to get seriously hurt. I think I need a moment away that's more than just a couple of hours. I've talked with some friends, and plans have been made for a girls' weekend at the beach, and we can go next month. If I can just tell these girls I'm in, it'll give me something to look forward to for the next several weeks and maybe, just maybe, I won't kill one of the kids and end up in jail."

When Katie has come to me with this kind of request, there are two possible reactions I can have. Reaction #1 is something like this: "Look, you want to go to the beach with some girls. I get it. But when you leave, I have to do both *my job* and *your job* as well. And it really wears me out. And I don't ask you to step in and do my job for me so I can take some time away. So, basically, no, I don't think this is such a good idea."

That's one possible response. Honestly, it's a natural response springing forth from my sinful, selfish nature.

The second possible reaction is unnatural, but much better for my spouse and my marriage. Reaction #2 is, "Absolutely. I know this is good for you. It will recharge your batteries and help you be a better wife and mom. I'm happy to do it."

You're probably assuming that since I'm a pastor and writing a book on marriage that reaction #2 has been my standard response to these kind of requests. Your assumption is wrong. As I write these words, I recognize how it just makes sense that I should react that way; however, I'm also a very selfish person.

I wake up each morning, look in the mirror, and ask the person staring back at me, "What can I do to serve you today?" If something comes along that doesn't meet that end goal, then, my first inclination is to push against whatever that is.

> *It's in the context of marriage that we are most tempted to act out of selfish ambition and place our own interests above the interests of our spouse.*

This natural reaction isn't best for our marriage. This selfish approach isn't good for *any* marriage. The healthiest marriages are the ones where each spouse asks, "How can I best serve my partner?," rather than, "How can I get my way today?"

Two verses in the New Testament book of Philippians speak to the approach spouses should take with one another: "*Do nothing out of selfish ambition or vain conceit. Rather, in humility value others above yourselves, not looking to your own interests but each of you to the interests of the others*" (Philippians 2:3-4). While this passage addresses all of our relationships, I think its greatest applicability may just be between husbands and wives. It's in the context of marriage that we are most tempted to act out of selfish ambition and place our own interests above the interests of our spouse. When one partner acts in this self-focused manner, the other is tempted to do so as well.

It's similar to a couple of small children playing together and having fun. They seem to be getting along just fine, when suddenly one child decides he wants the toy of the other child. He takes it, then the other child snatches it back. The first child screams and hits the second. The second child cries and throws the toy at the head of the first. By this point, parents have entered the room and see one child with blood streaming down his forehead, and the other child screaming like his hair's on fire. Mom and Dad loudly ask, "What just happened?!?" With arms outstretched and fingers pointed at the noses of the other, the two children shout in unison: "He started it!"

This same sort of escalation happens in the marriage relationship. What begins as one careless word is met with a snappy response, which is matched with a scathing critique, which then leads to tears, yelling, or stone-cold silence. Perhaps bitterness forms or some passive-aggressive retaliation is planned. The power struggle continues and each asks, "What can I do to get my way? How can I get my spouse to bend to my will?"

That is, until one spouse or the other says, "Enough. I'm going to heed the words of Philippians 2. I'm willing to put your interests above my own." Then, the ice begins to thaw and hearts start to soften.

Ironically, the happiest individuals are the ones who take the approach of putting their husband or wife first. When we go against this natural bent within us and operate in this non-instinctive fashion, then we are actually serving ourselves as well. Our spouse and our marriage is happier and healthier, thus making our own lives better.

Here's the challenge: consider how you can give 100% in

your marriage, and expect your husband or wife to give 0%. I realize the pushback against this way of thinking: "He will run all over me! She'll have it so easy and won't do anything!"

Maybe. Or maybe your selfless acts, your kindhearted words, and your magnanimous spirit will completely change your spouse and your marriage.

It may just need to start with you.

CHAPTER 6

THE DREADED "D" WORD

Marriage Truth #6:
Your marriage will have really low points.

~ KATIE ~

Looking back, I can't believe I actually uttered the word, "divorce." I'm pretty sure I didn't mean it when I said it. I think it was either just my overly emotional reaction to whatever he'd said, or my attempt at getting him to take me seriously. Or perhaps a combination of the two. As the word came out of my mouth, I felt shocked. Like I was outside of my body, and someone else was controlling my vocal cords. It's not that I'd been thinking about divorce in the previous days or weeks. This was not something I'd ever considered to be an option. On the day we married, I made a commitment. I had every intention of honoring the words I'd spoken to him.

However, things weren't going as I'd expected. Not even close. I knew then and I know now that he loves me, but sometimes he's just so out of tune with my feelings. Especially at that particular point in our marriage. We'd had several big changes to our lives: we'd just moved back to the United States from living overseas; he'd started a job as the pastor of a church; we were doing a complete overhaul of a house we'd purchased; I was living in a new place trying to make new friends. I needed someone to talk to about my feelings, my frustrations, and my worries. When we married, I assumed (and I think rightly so) that he would be the one who would listen to me more than anyone else. That he would get me, know me, and understand my thoughts and emotions. I honestly believed that he would know when I needed a hug, or when to just listen instead of offering advice, or when to actually offer some words of wisdom and help me figure out what to do. I expected my husband to be my best friend in the world and the one I wanted to go to first for emotional support.

It's not that this expectation was unreasonable. When we dated, he was an amazing conversationalist. He would talk on the phone with me for hours about anything and everything. He listened to me complain about some trivial problem or an issue I was having at work. He seemed interested in everything I had to say, and was always ready to offer just the right words to make me feel better.

Even during our first year or two of marriage, things were so much better. Virtually every week he would stop at the grocery store and purchase a bouquet of fresh flowers for me. When we were dating, he heard me comment on how much I love Stargazer Lilies. Almost every week, on the kitchen table in the tiny house where we lived, there would be a fresh arrangement of flowers featuring Stargazer Lilies.

About three months after we married, we went one Saturday to Southpark Mall in Charlotte. I think we'd met some friends for dinner at a restaurant, and then afterwards decided to walk around the mall for a little while. We went into J. Crew, and there I saw a sweater I really liked. Unfortunately, it was $120 for the sweater, and I just couldn't justify that purchase. I knew it would go on sale at the end of the season, and I figured I'd wait until then and hopefully they'd still have my size.

The next week I came home from work one evening and saw a present sitting on our kitchen table. "It's for you," he said, handing me the box.

"What's the occasion?" I asked, trying to remember if I'd missed some special day in our relationship, like the anniversary of our first date or the first time we'd kissed.

"No occasion. Just thought of you today and got this for you." I opened the box, and there was the $120 sweater from J. Crew. "I saw how much you liked it, and I didn't want you to have to wait until the end of winter to be able to wear it. Plus, I think you'll look absolutely beautiful in it."

I was so happy that night. Not just because of the sweater (although it was a wonderful surprise) but because he thought of me and because of the words he spoke. He knew how to fill my emotional tank, and he did it so well.

However, in this new season of our marriage, I was getting zilch from him. When he came home in the evenings, he just seemed exhausted. Questions about his day or what was happening at the church were met with grunts or flippant one word answers. "*Fine.*" "*Good.*" "*Uh-huh.*" He wanted to eat dinner, watch a little television, and then go to bed. Sharing about his day wasn't at the top of his priority list.

This was so different from our first year of marriage. Then, he was a student pastor, and he would talk to me about retreats he was planning or ask me about the message he was preparing for a student worship service. He seemed to truly value my opinion, and he was eager for my input.

Now, for some reason, he'd suddenly cut me out. He never wanted to talk to me about "church stuff." He didn't ask my opinions on sermon topics or discuss plans he was making. He might occasionally tell me a funny story about something that happened at work. When he did, I desperately hung on to every word because I was finally getting a small piece of him back. I felt so hurt at being shut out of his world. We'd spent our time in Charlotte "doing student ministry" together. I helped with girls' small groups; I went on every trip and retreat; I listened to every Wednesday night sermon and Sunday school lesson. Then, we moved overseas to Italy to serve as missionaries together. We were very much partners in ministry. It felt like I'd been by his side for so many steps along the way, only now to be suddenly dismissed from my role.

> *I needed my old husband back,*
> *but it wasn't happening.*
> *He had cut me out of his life.*

Later I would learn what he was doing. He wanted to protect me from ever feeling angry or bitter towards the church. He didn't want his struggles to affect my time in worship or serving the church. He was careful to tell me the good and only the edges of anything bad, normally with a positive spin. Now, looking back, I'm thankful that he was guarding my heart from a road many pastor's wives have traveled, where their husband's job actually damages their spiritual life rather than drawing them closer to God.

I now understand how his silence protected me in the long run, helping me to truly love our church with a deep affection. He made sure I didn't allow his struggles to become my own or cause bitterness to grow within me.

Now, I get it. Then, not so much. I was mad, hurt, and lonely. I needed my old husband back, but it wasn't happening. I felt as if we were two people living under the same roof, but with no emotional connection.

So, yeah, I said the word. The dreaded word. "Maybe," I said, "we should just get a divorce. Maybe we'd both be happier that way."

He shut down. I could see the tears forming in his eyes, but he became suffocatingly silent. He walked away, and I'm not sure if we ever finished that conversation. In fact, until I read the next chapter, I never really knew what he thought as I said those words. We never fully discussed all that we needed to talk through that day. At the time, the emotions were just too raw. We did, however, make a promise to one another: We would never mention the "D word" again in our marriage.

We've learned a lot since then. One of the key truths we've come to understand is that it's okay to have some days when marriage is a major struggle. It doesn't mean that we married the wrong person or that we are doomed and heading to the lawyer's office to file divorce papers. We are both human. We miscommunicate. We say things we don't really mean. Sometimes, we unfairly take out our frustrations on one another. We can both be selfish. Outside circumstances can put a lot of pressure on our marriage. Some days, quite frankly, can be tough.

However, we've grown from these experiences and learned that, when handled the right way, a difficult season can actually lead to a stronger, healthier marriage.

Kevin writes about this in the next chapter. If your marriage is in a rough patch right now, it doesn't mean it's over. Keep praying, talking, and working hard on your marriage. On the other side of this, God has something beautiful in store for you both.

CHAPTER 7

THE "D" WORD, PART 2

Marriage Truth #7:
Even at rock bottom, don't give up!

~ KEVIN ~

I think I was feeling a mixture of shock, hurt, and anger, all wrapped into one big tangled web of emotion. I could sense a physical change within me. Like riding a roller coaster and climbing that first gigantic hill. It felt like that moment when the cars are beginning to crest, just before they release and start racing down the tracks. My heart had moved somewhere into my stomach, or my stomach had moved into my throat, or something like that. I could feel the tears beginning to form, puddling around my eyes. Not overflowing and streaming down my cheeks, but enough to blur my vision.

I knew things had not been going well. Frankly, I was under a lot of stress, and she just didn't get it. This was my first experience serving as a lead pastor. That alone would have been overwhelming enough, but I was also having to pastor a wounded, hurting church. The previous pastor had resigned a year prior to my coming and started a brand new church in our community. Hundreds of individuals had left the church I now pastored to join him in this new ministry.

This caused constant comparisons. People loved to tell me what his church was doing and how they were growing. While most who left our church and joined that ministry did so before my arrival, several families did so *after* I became the pastor. This was something I never expected. They stayed at the church during the interim period, saying they were waiting to see who the new pastor would be before making a decision about staying or leaving. Truthfully, though, they'd already decided that they were leaving, but wanted to exit more gracefully by waiting until the new pastor came and everything was more settled. Then, they would feel like they had permission to leave. I had numerous meetings where individuals said, "Pastor, it's not you. We just need to do what is best for our family." I believed them, I think. The church could've hired Andy Stanley or Matt Chandler, and they would've still left, having one foot out the door before the new pastor arrived. Surely the problem wasn't me or my leadership.

Or... truthfully... maybe it *was* me. If only the church would've hired a pastor with more experience. Or one who was a better preacher. Or a better leader. Perhaps those families would've stayed. I wasn't exactly sure, but I was dealing with this issue on almost a weekly basis.

Additionally, there were extremely challenging issues with our staff. I suddenly had nine or ten employees who had been through the explosion of a church split, somehow managed to hang on during the interim period, then told they would be serving under a young, very inexperienced pastor. As I later learned, most believed my hiring to be a bad decision. They thought the Pastor Search Team had underestimated the need for a more seasoned pastor to manage the church's difficult situation. Several on our staff believed I wouldn't last long as pastor. I would either become frustrated and leave, or be asked to find another place of employment.

Most days, I agreed with their views. On paper, the leadership's decision to bring on a young pastor didn't make sense. I was severely unqualified for the role. The challenges seemed like a massive, insurmountable mountain, and my climbing experience was limited. I felt absolutely overwhelmed.

During my first few months as pastor, our weekly worship attendance declined slightly due to the exit of those who'd made their decision to leave after the church settled on a pastor. Fortunately, this didn't affect our giving. My guess is that most of those families had already dramatically reduced or ceased their giving altogether. I'm pretty sure their wallets left the church before their feet. While this marginal decline in attendance was discouraging, it wasn't nearly as stressful as what happened next.

The Great Recession.

One year after beginning my ministry at this church, the entire economy came to a screeching halt. Our giving (as was the case with churches everywhere) declined significantly. When people are losing their jobs and their homes, charitable giving is among the first expenses to cut. I knew many families in our church who were struggling just to make ends meet. I didn't expect them to give, and even if I'd pushed them on the issue, I'm not sure they could've done much at all. It was the whole blood / turnip thing.

We began cutting everything we could in our church budget. All the extras. The fluff people had added during the good years. Subscriptions to online services, advertising, cleaning, landscaping. We trimmed any and all excess fat. Employees had to pay a greater portion of the healthcare premiums. No raises were given for a couple of years. Every budget area was examined and any requests for spending were put through a battery of questions.

On more than one occasion, our financial administrator came to me on a Friday morning and said, "If we don't have a good offering on Sunday, we won't be able to make payroll next week." She'd already processed the payroll, but knew we didn't currently have the funds in the bank to cover the checks. Without a good offering to deposit first thing on Monday morning, our employees' paychecks would only be worth the paper they'd been printed on. Thankfully, we never once missed a payroll, but

I spent a lot of Saturdays worrying that the following week's staff meeting would be quite sour as I explained why they'd received *insufficient funds* notices regarding their last deposit.

> **She** expected me to be this emotional well she could draw from whenever she needed, but I was completely drain**ed**.

Added to all of this pressure was the fact that we'd just moved into a new home, and there were personal financial struggles as well. Paying the mortgage, remodeling the house, buying furniture for the home... there were a lot of weeks and months that our bank account balance would fall into the single digits.

Then Katie told me we were expecting our first child. We would be losing her income in a few months. Our already tight budget was about to get tighter. And her hormones were going crazy and she kept buying all this stuff for the baby. *Did this child really need thirty different outfits on the day she was born?* We needed to be saving this money, not spending it on clothes that would just be ruined by regurgitated milk!

She expected me to be this emotional well she could draw from whenever she needed, but I was completely drained. Sometimes she would think she was helping me by offering to talk through my problems. I didn't want to talk. I wanted a break. I needed some way to relax. She just didn't seem to get it. Looking back now, I wish I'd talked with her more. My silence only compounded the problems. However, at the time, opening up seemed to be too challenging. I was just overwhelmed.

So, yeah, I wasn't doing all the things I did when we dated and were first married. I wasn't buying flowers every week or staying up late to talk. And I certainly wasn't buying $120 sweaters as a surprise "just because I love you" gift. We needed that money for the mortgage payment. Or for all the dresses our first child would be wearing. I guess I understood why she wasn't as happy in our marriage as she'd been, but things certainly weren't all rainbows and unicorns for me, either.

Even so, I'd made a commitment, and divorce wasn't an option. Or, now, maybe it was. She brought it up. Perhaps this marriage wasn't worth saving. Maybe going our separate ways would be a lot easier.

Now, looking back, I'm so thankful we didn't give serious consideration to pulling the divorce lever. It was certainly a rough patch, and there were days we both felt like giving up. The word wouldn't have been uttered if we weren't really struggling with our marriage. Fortunately, it wasn't really an option.

However, maybe you *have* considered divorce. Perhaps, for you and your spouse, this has been or is currently an option. Maybe you are viewing this as a possible solution to your marriage problems.

Or perhaps you've never actually said the word, but you've imagined what life would be like if you were no longer married to your spouse. You've wondered whether or not life would be better or worse if you both just went your separate ways.

Or you've thought about the picture of your life if you'd

never married. Or if you'd married that other person. Would you be happier? Would your marriage to someone else have worked better?

Perhaps these have only been fleeting thoughts at various low points in your marriage. Maybe these ideas have run through your mind immediately after a big fight or after a few days of coolness between the two of you.

Or perhaps you *have* seriously considered divorce. You've thought hard about contacting that attorney and you've started to mentally make plans for a post-marriage existence. You and your spouse have honestly asked the question: Should we keep working on something that just doesn't seem to work?

Here's our encouragement to you: First of all, if you've had these thoughts, considerations, or conversations, you're not necessarily in a doomed marriage. You're just normal. Marriage can be very challenging, and during the hardest times our minds can wander down dangerous paths. Or our hearts begin to separate from this person we've vowed to love until death. Or, practical steps are made in the direction of divorce. If any of these apply or have applied to you and / or your spouse, then you are in a very normal marriage relationship.

Secondly, it is absolutely worth the effort. You may be in a rough patch right now. Or you've been in a dry season for quite some time. And you are wondering if the grass really is greener on the other side of your imaginary fence. The best thing you can do is to spend time watering your own lawn. What seems brown right now, in this season, will green up quickly when you give it the attention it needs. Don't give up now; it may be that your big breakthrough is just around the corner.

> *Don't give up now; it may be that your big breakthrough is just around the corner.*

If you're holding this book, then hopefully you have no intention of quitting. Reading and going through these exercises may just be the irrigation your marriage needs right now. We understand. We've been there and walked on the brown, crunchy grass of our own marriage. It can be really hard, but it can be so beautiful when you come out of the dry season and experience the lush, fulfilling intimacy of a marriage that has survived the difficult times.

We are pulling for you!

CHAPTER 8

TEAM US

Marriage Truth #8:
A healthy marriage requires teamwork.

~ KATIE ~

Although I can't remember when we heard this phrase and the lessons behind it, there was a point when we began talking about this certain idea and applying it to our marriage. The phrase is "Team Us." The concept behind this mentality is that I am never to be in competition with my spouse. My husband and I are a team. What is good for him is good for the team; therefore, it's good for me.

WHY TOOTHPASTE MATTERS

I graduated from the University of North Carolina at Chapel Hill. Living in this place filled with basketball fanatics, I drank every drop of the Carolina blue Kool-Aid. Now, years later, I spend many winter evenings and Saturday afternoons yelling at the television; either in disgust at the poor performance of my beloved Tarheels, or in great jubilation after a victory, especially if it happens to be against that sinister school in Durham with an ugly blue devil as their mascot.

With only five guys on the court at any one time, here is what I've learned: if one of our players has a great night, it likely means victory for the team. If just one guy is hitting lots of three-pointers, that alone might get the win for the team. Or if another player is having the defensive game of his life, it may just be the key to defeating our opponent. When one member of the team plays well, it benefits the team, and thus every individual on the team. They all pull for the success of their teammates because they understand this principle well: when one succeeds, they all succeed.

Athletes understand this, but married couples so often fail to live in this same way. Honestly, I've forgotten so many times to apply this concept in our marriage. I get frustrated with him or upset about something not going my way, and I attack my teammate. I begin to view him as the competitor instead of working with him and attacking the problem.

As mentioned in an earlier chapter, I enjoy going out to dinner with friends. I have a lot of weeks where 90% of my dialogue is with our four children, especially if Kevin has night meetings and isn't with us in the evenings. When this happens, I crave (or perhaps badly *need*) some adult conversation. Going to dinner with several girlfriends is the perfect prescription to cure this malady.

Based upon the length of our dinners, my friends seem to have the same need. Three and four hour meals are not unusual at all. Many times we have found ourselves still seated at our table as the waiter politely informs us that the restaurant is closing and asks us if we wouldn't mind taking our conversations to the benches located outside.

These long dinners and ensuing discussions outside wouldn't normally cause any issues in my marriage...*except*...Kevin has a really difficult time going to sleep if I'm not home. When I've asked him why, he's told me that it's a mixture of concern that I've arrived home safely and his own difficultly sleeping when anything is out of the norm. Many nights I've come home very late, only to find him still awake and more than a little frustrated with me, pleading with me to quickly go through my nighttime makeup-removal routine so that he can finally go to sleep.

Initially, his attitude *really* irritated me. As a 30-something year old adult, I shouldn't have a curfew. If I and my grown-up mom friends want to stay out a little late and talk, so what? It's not like we're at a dance club or bar having guys hit on us. We're closing down Olive Garden or sitting at a Fro-Yo store, laughing and filling each other's conversational tanks. Why in the world would he act so put out with me over something as innocent as these late night outings with friends?

Finally, it hit me. If he's really having trouble going to sleep, and I'm keeping him up late, then he'll struggle the next day in his studying, writing, meetings, or whatever he's facing in his job. He's not going to be as well-equipped to tackle whatever challenges his day throws at him. This in turn will hurt *Team Us*, and won't be good for me as well.

> *What is good for my spouse = good for the team = good for me.*

So, I've asked friends to meet earlier for dinners. Or go more often but not stay out as late. I want to do everything in my power to help my husband be happier and healthier and more well rested. Why? Because what is good for my spouse = good for the team = good for me.

When you view your husband or wife as a teammate, it changes how you approach conflict. If there is an issue, then it becomes my responsibility to work alongside my teammate to attack the problem together. For example, one time I said something like, "Hey, I understand the difficulty you have in going to sleep. Would you rather me go to dinner with the girls twice this month and be home earlier each night rather than just once but coming in late?" His reply: "Absolutely. That works much better."

When I took the approach of working *alongside him* rather than *against him*, the solution to this issue seemed to come much easier. We attacked the problem, not one another. The principle once again proved to be true: What is good for my spouse = good for the team = good for me.

To build a team mentality, we've tried to live by three rules.

In our experience, the more we're able to follow these rules, the better our relationship.

1. FIGHT FAIR

When conflict begins to rear its ugly head, there is a great temptation to pull out all the ammunition and use every dirty trick in the book. I have a very bad habit of using extreme language in our disagreements:

- "You always act this way."
- "You've never once said a nice thing to me."
- "You just think I'm the most awful person in the world."

Statements like these are never helpful and certainly don't encourage working together as a team to resolve the issue. I've had to learn to tone down my rhetoric (and many times my volume as well) and speak more reasonably. "The statement you made earlier really hurt my feelings" is much better than, "You always make statements that hurt my feelings." The latter is not only untrue, but typically serves to escalate the conflict.

We've also both been guilty of bringing up past sins, mistakes, and failures of the other into current conflicts:

- "This is just like the time you embarrassed me in front of my friends."

- "I still haven't gotten over what you did to me two years ago."
- "Sure, I was wrong, but this is just like what you did to me last month."

While sometimes these previous situations need to be discussed (especially if there are still lingering hurts), it's best not to drag out all the old fights in the middle of a new fight. Again, this does little to solve the conflict, and typically causes your spouse to give their own version of historical events as well.

Fighting fair also means severely curtailing your desire to interrupt and / or not listen to your spouse's side of the conversation. While I have the bad habit of jumping in and interrupting Kevin in the middle of what he's saying, he's sometimes guilty of only half listening to me while forming a stinging rebuttal in his head. Both approaches are wrong. As much as it goes against your natural way of fighting, really try to listen to your spouse. Remember, you're a team, together attacking the conflict.

2. GIVE THE BENEFIT OF THE DOUBT

I would venture to guess that more than half of our conflicts have revolved around misunderstandings, miscommunications, or careless words spoken at an inopportune moment. There have been times that either my hormones were going crazy or I'd just had a crummy day, and Kevin made a casual comment that really upset me. He certainly didn't mean to hurt me. Maybe it was somewhat thoughtless, but normally I would've just let it go. However, in that moment, it stung, and I snapped at him.

This happened several times during my two pregnancies, when I was gaining weight exponentially and riding the hormone roller coaster. If we were at a restaurant, he might flippantly say, "Wow, you ordered a lot. Are you sure you're going to eat all of that food?" He was concerned that we were spending too much money on food that would be left uneaten. All I heard was, "You're a fat pig." Thus, my reply would be something like, "I'm carrying YOUR baby; YOU did this to me; and *by-God* I'll order and eat the entire right side of this menu if that's what I want to do!"

I'm not sure if it ever went exactly like that, but you get the picture. We've both been guilty of assuming the worst about a statement or action of our partner, rather than giving the benefit of the doubt. We all misspeak at times. All of us, at times, have neglected to call and give our spouse an update on our status. We've forgotten to mention that thing we committed to doing, or added an event to the calendar without informing our teammate.

In our own marriage, this team rule has been invaluable. Beginning with the assumption that the other meant no harm and possessed no ulterior motive has prevented potential blow-ups or quickly ended our arguments. Again, this goes against our natural instincts. You want to roll your eyes and tear into your spouse for — *once again* — forgetting to do that thing or making that really insensitive comment. However, she is your teammate. He is your teammate. Give them the benefit of the doubt and then work to solve the problem together.

3. SHOW GRACE... AND LOTS OF IT.

Let's face it: none of us will always fight fair. In our marriage, we probably violate our team rules as much as we follow them. Which is why we desperately need this third rule: Show grace. Often. Lavishly. Give it again and again. You will fail and your spouse will fail. To live up to expectations, or to say the right things, or to consider the other's feelings. We all blow it from time to time. We've discovered that the more we are able to say the phrases, "I'm sorry," and "I forgive you," the healthier our marriage.

My suspicion is that the same is true for you and your spouse. When you are able to show exorbitant amounts of grace to one another, your marriage will thrive. Do this for your teammate, and hopefully they will do the same for you.

The next time you have a conflict with your spouse, hopefully this chapter will immediately come to mind. As the tension builds and you are tempted to lob a few verbal grenades, think about how you can best play the role of a good teammate. What can you do to attack the problem instead of your spouse? If you will approach your disagreements with a team mentality, you'll see your marriage becoming much stronger.

CHAPTER 9

WHY BOTHER?

Marriage Truth #9:
Your marriage is not primarily about you.

~ KATIE ~

Why did you get married? Or, why do you want to get married?

You may answer, "Because we were / are in love." Great. But you certainly don't have to get married to be in love. You were in love before you made vows to one another. The marriage ceremony didn't change the way you two felt about one another, did it?

You may say, "Because we wanted to raise a family together." Again, that is completely possible without being married.

Numerous couples today live together and have children without going through the trouble of getting a marriage license and having a judge or pastor pronounce them to be husband and wife.

Maybe you say, "Because I wanted the ceremony and the pictures and for all of my friends to get together and serve as bridesmaids / groomsmen and to have the big celebration and to get lots of nice presents."

Okay, maybe that is a good reason. I guess you could do all those things without actually getting married, but you would have difficulty explaining to your friends and family why they were paying money for dresses and tuxedos and gifts if you weren't really saying the vows.

However, let's face it: Practically speaking, you don't have to be married to live together, purchase a house, have children, celebrate holidays, go on vacation, or pretty much anything else married couples do or share together.

So why bother? Why did you or should you go through the marriage ceremony and repeat vows to one another?

If you are not a follower of Christ, I'm so thankful you are reading this book. I believe it will help you in your marriage, even if you do not follow Jesus or believe in the existence of God. Simply discussing your expectations and communicating with your spouse will help your relationship grow stronger and your marriage thrive.

However, if you are a follower of Christ, there is something you need to know about your marriage. It's not about you. Your marriage is not primarily about your happiness. If you grew up going to church, you've likely heard this before. Pastors and Sunday School teachers have talked about marriage being more than just an institution ordained by God for our own joy and pleasure. Marriage, they have proclaimed, is about growing and shaping us into more Jesus-like individuals. "Your marriage," I've heard, "isn't primarily about your happiness, but about your holiness."

I agree, to an extent. In fact, I desire both happiness and holiness in my marriage. My marriage has brought me great happiness and has certainly made me a more holy person. However, neither is the main point of my marriage. Or yours. Really, your marriage is not primarily about you at all. Or your spouse. God did not ordain marriage primarily for us. God gave the institution of marriage chiefly for a reason outside of the husband and wife.

How do I know this? Because of what I read in Ephesians 5 about the roles of husbands and wives. This book was originally a letter written by this Christian leader named Paul. In explaining the way the marriage relationship should work, Paul wrote:

Wives, submit yourselves to your own husbands as you do to the Lord. (22)

In the next paragraph, he addressed the men:

Husbands, love your wives, just as Christ loved the church and gave himself up for her. (25)

I understand the tension around these verses and the controversy regarding "male headship" in a marriage versus the egalitarian view. Putting that aside for just a moment, consider the radical nature of these statements. More than an org chart for marriage, these verses are a call for husbands and wives to place the needs of their spouses above their own. To be so radically committed to one another that they are always acting in ways that benefit the other.

Wives, respect your husbands. Even when you think he doesn't deserve respect, show it. Give him every benefit of the doubt, listen to his opinion, never publicly criticize him, treat him with great admiration. Show him the same respect you show to Jesus.

Husbands, love your wives. Put her needs above your own. Remember what Jesus did for the church? For you? He suffered and gave his life. That's how much he loves you. Love your wife with the same kind of sacrificial love.

> **More than an org chart for marriage, these verses are a call for husbands and wives to place the needs of their spouses above their own.**

Did Paul write these words primarily because this is how a marriage works best? Sure, that's part of it. I can't imagine a marriage operating in this way and the couple splitting up. A wife who treats her husband with that kind of respect and a husband who loves his wife that sacrificially will likely have a thriving, happy marriage.

However, that's not the principal purpose in marriage. Your marriage is not primarily about your happiness or even your holiness. More than anything else, your marriage is about the gospel. Notice what Paul wrote in that same section on marriage:

This is a profound mystery—but I am talking about Christ and the church. (32)

Marriage, according to this verse, is designed to be a reflection of the relationship between Christ and the church. More specifically, Christian marriage was given by God as a way to illustrate the gospel message to those who do not know Christ.

You and your spouse interact with numerous individuals who may have no interest in reading a Bible or going to a church. But, they work with you, or your spouse, or they live in your neighborhood, or their children play soccer with your children. They may have never *heard* the gospel, but your marriage is a perfect opportunity to *show* them the gospel. In a world where husbands love sports more than their wives, where wives publicly criticize their husbands, where spouses constantly complain about their marriage, and where selfish pursuits are common, your marriage has the potential to grab the attention of those around you. These individuals will sit up and take notice of how you treat one another.

Think about the ways most marriages operate. The divorce rate in our country is 50%. This statistic has been true during all of my lifetime. Half of marriages are so broken that one or both partners decide to call it quits. The marriage reaches the point that, at least in their minds, there is nothing left to salvage.

> *Your marriage is not primarily about your happiness or even your holiness. More than anything else, your marriage is about the gospel.*

Out of the other 50%, how many of those marriages are thriving? How often do we see husbands placing their jobs, or sports, or their hobbies above the needs of their spouse? How many wives are quick to criticize their husbands when they are hanging out with their girlfriends? Think about the numerous couples who live together and raise their children, but their conversations and interactions are all centered around the business of the household? Perhaps they are staying together for financial reasons, or for the sake of the children, or simply because they don't want to be alone. But, there's no respect and there's certainly no love.

This kind of marriage has become the norm for so many. Marriages ending in divorce and marriages with scant love and affection are common.

So, when a husband loves his wife as Christ loves the church, and a wife shows the same respect to her husband that she shows to the Lord, the marriage becomes a bright light in a dark world. People will naturally ask, "Why is he so devoted and loving towards his wife? Why doesn't she join in with us while we criticize our husbands? How is it that they treat each other so well?"

The answer: "Because they get it. Their marriage isn't just about them. They have worked hard on their relationship because they understand that their marriage is to be a picture of the gospel to those who desperately need Jesus. They try their best to show unconditional love to one another in order to help people understand the unconditional love of God through Christ. Their desire is to truly honor God with their marriage."

However, it can't be just for show. People will see right

through an act. But when you wake up each morning and say, "God, please help me love my wife today with the same unconditional love that you have shown me," or, "God, give me the ability to love and respect my husband with the same love and respect I show you," then I truly believe God will answer those prayers.

Here is the icing on the cake: your marriage isn't about you — *however* — when it operates in this way, life is just better. This is the great irony of marriage. When we take the focus off of our own happiness and look to the needs of our spouse, not only does our marriage proclaim the gospel, we get that whole happiness thing as well. It's similar to the message Jesus gave regarding salvation: *For whoever wants to save their life will lose it, but whoever loses their life for me will find it* (Matthew 16:25). In your marriage, the more you make it about your spouse, the happier you'll be.

Sounds pretty good, doesn't it?

CHAPTER 10

LIVING AS AN ANCESTOR

Marriage Truth #10:
Your marriage will leave a legacy.

~ KEVIN ~

Every one of us will leave a legacy. This we know with complete certainty. When our time on this earth is finished, the way we lived will continue to impact those still alive. None are exempt from this reality. The decisions we make in the days, months, and years we are alive will have an ongoing effect long after we are gone.

The only real question you need to ask is this: *What kind of legacy will I leave?* Your life will influence others either positively or negatively. Those who come after you will either benefit from the decisions you made, or your actions and words will continue to have a detrimental effect, even after you are gone. The legacy you leave behind really, really matters in the lives of those still living.

If you are married and have children, your legacy will most greatly impact your children. Again, the only question is *what kind* of legacy you will leave. Most of us tend to limit what we think about leaving behind to our children to the financial realm, whether it is a small or large inheritance.

However, when you view your legacy from God's perspective, you will discover that money is a *very minor* ingredient of your legacy. From an eternal perspective, focusing solely on finances is extremely near-sighted. You will miss the much greater, far more impactful component of your legacy.

Notice the following instruction to the people of Israel found in the Old Testament book of Exodus:

> *...for I, the Lord your God, am a jealous God, punishing the children for the sin of the parents to the third and fourth generation of those who hate me, but showing love to a thousand generations of those who love me and keep my commandments. (Exodus 20:5-6)*

This same phrase — *punishing to the third and fourth generation of those who hate me; showing love to a thousand generations of those who love me* — is repeated on three other occasions in the Old Testament (Numbers 14:18; Exodus 34:7; Deuteronomy 5:9) almost exactly word for word. This principle, that generations will inherit from their parents both the *good* and *bad*, is seen in dozens of places in both the Old and New Testaments. Each passage and verse reaffirms that the most important legacy we can leave is a *spiritual one*. A spiritual legacy is one which will impact your children for the rest of their earthly and eternal lives. Your children will receive both the blessings of your good choices and the curses of your bad choices.

> *Your children will receive both the blessings of your good choices and the curses of your bad choices.*

This feels like a lot of pressure, doesn't it? Almost like we are expected to be perfect in every decision we make and in every word we utter. I read these words in Exodus and two emotions seem to simultaneously overwhelm me: guilt and worry. I feel the burden of guilt over the selfish decisions I've made and how they have affected and will continue to affect my children, grandchildren, and all my greats. Additionally, I worry about my past and future wrong decisions, and the impact those will have on the generations coming after me.

Fortunately, there is a truth that overcomes my guilt and

worry: God's grace is far greater than my sin. These verses aren't given to cause us shame or worry. Rather, they are meant to highlight the legacy principle. None of us live on an island. Our lives will shape those who come behind us — and most of all our direct descendants.

Practically speaking, here is how this looks: **Live your life today as an ancestor.** Make decisions now as one who will be remembered as a grandparent, a great-grandparent, or a great-great-grandparent. Live out your present days knowing that you will be an ancestor to those who are yet to come. Ask yourself: "What do I want my legacy to be? What impact do I want to have? What kind of lives do I want my great-greats to be living?"

This principle has profoundly impacted my marriage. The way I treat Katie today impacts how my sons will treat their wives, and how their sons will treat their wives, and even how my great-grandchildren will treat their wives. Our marriage will impact my daughters' views of their own marriages, and then their children, and then the children of those children. My approach to our marriage will leave a legacy which will be felt for generations to come.

Katie and I had a whirlwind dating and engagement period in 2004 and 2005. We'd dated previously, and as we've often said, it was the "right person, wrong time." We were in different cities and different stages of life, and so we split up for about two years. When we began dating again, things moved quickly. Within just a few months, I'd purchased a ring. A few weeks later, we were engaged. Four months later, we were married. She's reminded me often that four months wasn't nearly enough time to plan a wedding. I've reminded her that she's a natural procrastinator and even if we'd set the wedding two years after the engagement, she would've waited until the last four months to plan it all anyway.

During the first year of our marriage, we lived in a small rental house in Charlotte, North Carolina. The next year we moved to Rome, Italy as employees of the International Mission Board. We lived in Rome for a year before returning to the United States, where I began serving as the pastor of Northway Church in Macon, Georgia.

Those first couple of years were unbelievably exciting. Everything was new. Our marriage was new. We lived in a new house. Then we quit our jobs and began working for a new company. We moved to a new city in a new country, lived in a new culture, and learned a new language. We were able to travel while living in Italy to cities throughout Europe: Venice, Florence, Naples, Paris, Lisbon, Vienna, Barcelona. Every day was a new adventure with our new partner exploring new places.

Moreover, we were young and free. Although we didn't (and probably couldn't) appreciate it at the time, not having children allowed us to go and do with ease. We spent many Saturday afternoons walking around the city of Rome, exploring churches and historic landmarks. Many evenings we would walk to a small, inexpensive restaurant just around the corner from our apartment and have a nice, quiet dinner together. We'd then walk home, exhausted from our day, and watch the latest episode of *Lost* we'd downloaded from iTunes (this was pre-Netflix and Hulu streaming days). We didn't have to worry about getting a baby sitter, changing diapers, or midnight feedings. We had a tremendous amount of freedom.

However, it was just the beginning of our marriage. Since that time, we've entered new, exciting chapters and encountered different challenges. Looking back, I've realized that our marriage could easily have been a star that burned brightly for a little while, but then flamed out after just a few years. As mentioned in an earlier chapter, this came closer to becoming reality than either of us ever imagined. We had some rough times. We've continued to have conflicts and challenges. But, our perspective has changed since those early years. Ecclesiastes 7:8 puts it this way: *The end of a matter is better than its beginning.* Something, anything, might begin with a lot of promise, passion, or success, but the true test of its effectiveness and impact can only be judged in the end.

This is how we view our marriage — with an end goal in mind. We want our marriage to leave a legacy for our children and the generations to come. The end goal is to not just make it, but to thrive and cross the finish line together, still holding hands. We want to look back on a marriage that, while far from perfect, was a tremendous blessing to us and to others. That is the legacy we desire to leave.

What about you? Is this a goal in your marriage? Are your decisions being made not just for the moment, but what impact they will have a century from now?

Whenever I am asked to officiate a wedding, I always meet

with the couple for premarital counseling. In our first session together, I try to paint a picture for them. Decades have passed, and they are sitting in rocking chairs on the front porch of their mountain home or beach house. They've raised children and retired from their jobs. They are enjoying grandchildren, traveling some, volunteering in their church, going to various doctor's appointments more than they'd like, and doing all the things a retired couple does together.

I have them imagine this moment, sitting next to one another, holding hands, and having time to reflect together on their marriage. "Perhaps you'll look back on fifty years together. Or sixty. Maybe more. As you are discussing this journey you've taken with each other, what do you think you'll say? What kinds of things do you hope you'll be able to talk about? How would you want to be able to describe your marriage?"

Then, after they've visualized themselves having this discussion, I'll say, "Start working towards that goal now. You won't just stumble into a marriage that is able to go the distance. Put in place now the things necessary for that rocking-chair scene to be what you want it to be. Think about your finances, your friends, how you treat one another, your church involvement... do the things now that will get you to the place of looking back on your marriage with great joy."

We all need to stop occasionally and consider this same rocking-chair scenario. Couples should look to see if they are heading in the right direction, or if there are course corrections that need to be made in their relationship.

What adjustments, if any, do you need to make in your own marriage? Think about your long term goals and the legacy you will leave. What do you want it to be? Begin today with the end in mind.

PART 2

REBOOT:
SIX WEEKS TO A
BETTER MARRIAGE

WEEK 1

YOUR BIGGEST BATTLE
Fighting the Money Struggle Together

Unless you are so incredibly wealthy that you never have to think about money, or so absolutely poor that there's nothing to fight over, you will have more disagreements over finances than anything else in your marriage. How to spend, when to spend, what to spend it on, why you didn't let me know you were going to spend that, why you spent so much, how much to save, if we save anything at all... the issues will be countless and you'll have many of the same fights numerous times. Money will be somewhere in the mix of at least half of your disagreements.

Managing this area of your lives takes work and intentionality.

WHY TOOTHPASTE MATTERS

The same passion that carried you through dating, engagement, and your honeymoon will not sustain you through the money fights. You need a battle plan, and you need it established early in your marriage.

The first thing you need to do as a couple is to make sure you're on the same page regarding your view of finances. There is a prayer about money that has guided our marriage for many years. This prayer is found in the book of Proverbs:

> *Two things I ask of you, Lord;*
>> *do not refuse me before I die:*
> *Keep falsehood and lies far from me;*
>> *give me neither poverty nor riches,*
>> *but give me only my daily bread.*
> *Otherwise, I may have too much and disown you*
>> *and say, 'Who is the Lord?'*
> *Or I may become poor and steal,*
>> *and so dishonor the name of my God. (Proverbs 30:7-9)*

There is so much wisdom in this prayer. Too many material possessions and a hefty bank balance can easily cause someone to forget God. This is one of the greatest reasons, in our culture today, so many people refuse to consider their need for God and salvation. "I've got a big house, a vacation home, three cars in the garage, nice clothes, and I never have to worry about food. What exactly do I need to be *saved* from?" Riches can easily keep us from realizing our need for God. It's why Jesus said, "*It's easier for a camel to go through the eye of a needle than for someone who is rich to enter the kingdom of God"* (Matthew 19:24; Mark 10:25; Luke 18:25). Jesus wasn't adding extra requirements for the wealthy person to gain salvation. He was simply pointing out the fact that money, and lots of it, is often a barrier between us and God.

The other part of this prayer on riches is just as important: "Lord, please keep me from poverty...otherwise I might resort to stealing and disobey you." While riches may cause one to *forget* God, poverty may lead to *dishonoring* God.

The prayer for your marriage might go something like this: "God, please give us enough. Not so much that we begin to drift away from you, and not so little that we are constantly fighting and/or consumed with money issues. Give us what we can handle within our marriage and family."

We get it: you may say, "Look, I'm not sure about that prayer. I think I'd rather pray for riches." However, we know plenty of couples who are financially prosperous, but their marriage is miserable. They'd trade their wealth for happiness in a heartbeat.

For the vast majority of couples, there are two parts to overcoming the financial struggle together. The first is getting on the same page regarding your view of money. Do you both have a biblical perspective on this issue? Is the love of money ruling your hearts? Are you and / or your spouse far too consumed with accumulating treasures on earth? The first part of your conversation regarding finances should focus on the purpose, benefits, and dangers of money.

Once you've discussed your view of money, the second part

of this battle is getting on the same page in how you will allocate the actual dollars in your bank account. Practically speaking, this is making sure you have communicated and are following through on the spending, saving, and tracking of your finances. This is not normally discussed in the dating / engagement period of your relationship. Truthfully, it's not the most exciting topic. Yet, a failure to synchronize your financial practices will cause great destruction in your marriage.

There are numerous tools available to assist you in this endeavor. From budgeting sites to spending apps, we are fortunate to have an abundance of resources literally at our fingertips. You and your spouse can download the same app onto your phone and easily track every penny spent, place the expenditure in a previously budgeted category, and quickly review your previous month's actual to budgeted income and expenses.

Over the years of our marriage, we've used a variety of different methods to assist us in tracking expenses. We began with pencil and paper, moved to a spreadsheet on the computer, then a budget app, and another budget app, back to an old school paper method, another app, etc.

We've also changed our family treasurer a number of times. Kevin began as the controller of the money, then it went to Katie, then both of us (that didn't work), then back to Kevin, then back to Katie and has stayed that way for several years. We've discovered that, in our relationship, it's best for one person to be paying the bills and managing our accounts.

The important thing for your relationship is not what you do, but making sure you are on the same page with how you do it. This is an area where you need to figure out what works, what doesn't work, and how to make adjustments when income and expenses change over the course of your marriage.

For some couples, this week's exercise won't take long. You've got a system that works well and you've been using it for years. You have few fights concerning money. You know what you have and how it's being spent. You have a savings plan, a paying-off-debt plan, and an emergency plan. Even if your income is a fraction of your neighbor's, you've figured out how to manage your money in a way that keeps stress at bay and arguments away from your marriage.

For others, your discussion will take a long while. If you've gone out to a restaurant to do this week's questions, you may want to order dessert and warn the waitress that you'll be there for a while. You have no financial plan. You've not discussed goals. Savings — what's that? You're living paycheck to paycheck, and your fights over money are constant.Talk through these questions and begin exploring resources to assist you in your money habits. Then, hopefully, you'll start turning your financial ship in a different direction.

QUESTIONS

1   How do you view money? How do you think I view money? Do you think I love money and / or stuff too much?

2   Do we have a budget? If not, when can we find time to create one? If so, do we need to review it?

3   What are our short-term financial goals? Is there any credit card debt we need to eliminate? Are there purchases we will need to make in this next year?

4   What are our long-term financial goals? When do we want to have our house mortgage paid off? Have we saved enough for retirement? Do we need to save for college tuition payments? Are there any other financial goals we need to discuss?

5   How can we best help each other stay on track to meet these financial goals?

6   If we were suddenly given $20,000, how would you want to spend it?

7   Are any of my spending habits negatively affecting our marriage? Our family? Our future?

8   Do any of your friends / my friends not support us in our financial goals? How can I / we manage these friendships better? What about our extended family members? Are they supporting us in our financial goals? Do we need to establish better boundaries in those relationships?

9   Are we currently tithing? If not, how can we start?

10 Do you have any completely frivolous things you dream of purchasing one day in the future? (a big trip, a sports car, jewelry, a boat, etc.)

WEEK 2

ALL IN THE FAMILY

Creating Healthy Boundaries and Connections

Marriage is designed to create new families. Jesus put it in these words: "A man will leave his father and mother and be united to his wife, and the two will become one flesh. So they are no longer two, but one flesh. Therefore what God has joined together, let no one separate" (Matthew 19:5-6).

In order for this new family to be created, the old families must be left. This doesn't mean the wife should ignore her parents or that the husband needs to cut his siblings out of his life. What it *does* mean is that each of them must have a new first priority. If you are married, your greatest human allegiance is to your spouse. S/he comes before your parents and your siblings. Your ultimate loyalty is to him. Your trust is in her. His needs come before the needs of your parents. Her needs come before the needs of your brothers or sisters.

Too often we see couples having a difficult time making this transition. They marry, but their primary loyalty remains with their parents, siblings, or other family members. He doesn't want to upset his mom, so he puts her needs above the needs of his wife. She turns to her father every time she needs advice, causing her husband to become jealous or feel inferior. The family wants and expects you to be at *their* home for the holidays, and the desire to please the family leads to one continuous fight.

Navigating these situations isn't always easy. Family dynamics can be quite challenging. However, you must begin with the premise that your spouse is your number one priority. If that is your foundational belief, then together you can work out your responses to any requests or demands of your families.

Likewise, when a couple marries, friendships are no longer your greatest priority. Again, this certainly doesn't mean you abandon friends. They were important relationships before you were married, and that doesn't change after marriage. You still want to talk to and spend time with these individuals.

However, these friendships cannot be more important than your marriage relationship. Too often we have seen unhealthy friendships cause division in marriages. It may be simply that a spouse spends far too much time with friends. He loves playing golf three days a week with the guys. She goes to dinner with girlfriends several nights each week. The spouse feels abandoned and less important than "the guys" or "the girls."

Or perhaps it's friendships that are unsupportive of the marriage. Her friends will criticize her husband, or make suggestions about how she could've done better, or his friends continually insist that the marriage won't last much longer. Their influence causes cracks to form in the relationship, and when difficulties arise between him and her, the suggestions of these friends cause far more harm than good.

Or, as happens too often, spouses remain close friends with members of the opposite sex after marriage. While it's fine to retain these friendships, it's unhealthy for a husband or wife to remain extremely close with members of the opposite sex. Before marriage, I (Katie) had close guy friends, and I (Kevin) had close friendships with girls. We talked on the phone, went to dinner, and hung out with these friends of the opposite sex.

After our marriage, however, those friendships took a backseat. We still value these relationships; we just understand the danger in being too close with a guy / girl who is not our spouse. When there are difficult seasons in the marriage (and every marriage will have those), turning to a member of the opposite sex for counsel, support, or just companionship can easily lead to feelings of affection. We know boundaries must be in place to protect our hearts and our marriage.

Finally, when you have children, your first priority is to your spouse, not your children. Again, this doesn't mean you ignore or neglect the needs of your kids. You love them dearly and would literally give your lives for them. You offer them support and encouragement. You want to protect them and provide for them. Your ultimate goal is to raise a child who grows into a mature, responsible adult. Through all of this, keep in mind that your spouse is your first priority, not the child(ren). One day (hopefully) your child(ren) will leave your home. Then they will meet and marry someone else. That person will then become their first priority, not you. This is why spouses often wait until the kids are out of the house before they divorce. Their marriage had been dead for years because they placed their kids before each other.

Quite ironically, in our observations, when the parents make *each other* their first priority, the children thrive. Children want to know that their parents really love each other and that their marriage is of first importance. This gives the children a strong sense of security. The relationship between Mom and Dad becomes their safe place, giving them the confidence they need as they go out into the world.

In your marriage, your spouse must come first; before other family members, before friends, and even before your own children. The two of you are "one." The interests and needs of your spouse are primary.

QUESTIONS

1   Do you think our relationships with parents / in-laws are good? Is there anything you would change in how we spend our time or communicate with them?

2   Do we have healthy relationships with other extended family members? Anything we need to change in how we relate with them?

3   Do we need to have better boundaries with family for holidays / birthdays?

4   Are there any friends of mine that you think get in the way of our marriage? What changes can I make that will help you feel more comfortable with this friendship?

5   Do you ever feel that you are "second place" to the kids? What can I do to change that?

6   Do you think we are disciplining our child(ren) correctly? Is there anything you think we should change?

7   How are we doing in raising our child(ren) to become (a) responsible adult(s)? Are we helping them develop and grow their faith in God? What can we do better?

8   Is there anything we should change in our parenting right now?

WEEK 3

BETWEEN THE SHEETS

Staying on the Same Page in the Bedroom

The Old Testament book *Song of Solomon* is all about a new-lywed couple *enjoying* their physical relationship with one an-other. Anyone who does not believe God created sex to be a pleasurable experience between a husband and wife has never read this book. God is pro-sex, pro-*enjoyment* of sex, and creat-ed it *as a gift to couples.*

Whenever I (Kevin) meet with engaged couples and tell them that sex will be one of their major fights, they always look at me like my dog does when I whistle at her. Heads cocked, confused expressions, and big cartoon question marks float over their heads. They just can't seem to understand how this wonderful, pleasurable act could ever lead to a fight.

Anyone who has been married more than a year or two (and especially those of you who have children) understand the problem. I can probably summarize it best with two words: *timing* and *frequency*. Certainly there are other issues that may enter into this area of your marriage, but most disagreements will revolve around when and how often. Again, engaged couples and newlyweds may have trouble understanding how this can possibly be. But throw in a newborn baby, a woman whose hormones still haven't come back anywhere close to normal, the stress of a job, a fight from earlier in the day, tension with the in-laws, self-consciousness about recently gained weight, and a thousand more external factors. He's ready, and she's just not in the mood. She's finally in the mood, and he's still at work. He gets home, and now she's tired and just wants to sleep. Again, *frequency* and *timing*.

Moreover, there are two different ways guys and girls approach sex. For guys, sex is 90% physical and 10% romance. For girls, it's the exact opposite. For guys, it can be as much a stress reliever as an act of romance. For girls, the emotional connection is just as important as the physical feelings. Because of the way we are differently wired, sex can easily become a source of conflict in a marriage.

For wives, the act of sex can actually be a way to help your husband spiritually. Notice what Paul wrote in his first letter to the church at Corinth: *Do not deprive each other except perhaps by mutual consent and for a time, so that you may devote your-selves to prayer. Then come together again so that Satan will not tempt you because of your lack of self-control* (I Corinthians 7:5).

A married couple not sleeping together has opened the door to temptation. This is especially true for men. A husband struggling for sexual fulfillment in the marriage will be tempted to look outside of the marriage to have his needs satisfied. This is typically through viewing pornography (a common struggle, even among Christian men) or even seeking out a physical relationship with another woman. While *no* affair is excusable, wives need to understand that the lack of a physical relationship at home will cause that temptation to be greater.

Thus, for wives, this is a way to minister to your husband and to help protect him from physical temptation outside of your marriage. If he is being tempted because his sex life at home has been shut down, even if he never acts on that temptation, it's probably not doing him a lot of good spiritually.

You may say, "You know, he's just not that romantic anymore," or, "His idea of romance now is to walk into the bedroom singing a Marvin Gaye song. He thinks that alone will get me to swoon and throw myself at him." You think he's not doing his part in this area, and you may be exactly right. However, consider *your part* and *your obligation* first. Let God deal with him on his obligation in this important part of your marriage relationship.

Husbands, you're likewise called to consider the needs of your spouse. For her, it's more than just sex. Romance, emotions, and security are all intertwined with the physical. While this also applies to guys, it's exponentially greater for females. Men and women are just wired differently in this area, and this difference can be a source of tension if you fail to meet her needs.

Therefore, work on being more romantic. This doesn't necessarily have to cost money or take much time on your part. It's an awareness and willingness to put forth the effort that will mean so much to her. When you leave the house in the morning to go your separate ways, give her a kiss that is more than a peck on the cheek. Send her a text in the afternoon letting her know that you're thinking about her. Either discover or rediscover what fills her emotional tank, and then pour into that area. If she loves a clean house, then clean. If she needs time with friends, then help make that happen. If she loves her morning coffee, pour the cup and bring it to her. You know (or, if you're engaged / newly married, will soon discover) what really makes her smile. Do those things. Say those things. Be present. Be attentive. Be considerate.

For many couples, this discussion may be slightly awkward, even if your sex life is good and healthy. Few are willing to discuss the details of this intimate part of your life. However, if you are frustrated (or even if you're not), sharing your feelings, desires, what works and what doesn't will bring you closer and help get you both on the same page in the bedroom.

QUESTIONS

1   Do you think our frequency of sex is enough? Ideally, how many times would you want to have sex in a week?

2   Name the 2-3 times we've had sex that were the most memorable for you.

3   What can I do either immediately before or during sex to make it more enjoyable for you?

4   What can I do in the twenty-four hours leading up to sex to make it more enjoyable for you?

5   Is there a certain time of the day you prefer to have sex?

6   Is there anything in our current schedule we need to change to make this part of our lives a priority?

7   If you were to give me a "cheat sheet" of what is most exciting to you, what would be on that list? Don't assume I just

know — help me understand how our intimate times together can be really fulfilling for you.

WEEK 4

GOOD FENCES MAKE GREAT MARRIAGES
Affair-Proofing Your Marriage

You most certainly know the name Billy Graham. Dr. Graham was considered to be "America's Pastor" for several decades. He met and prayed with numerous United States Presidents and other world leaders. He preached the gospel to millions — billions if you count his television and radio audiences.

Dr. Graham had a rule to protect his marriage and ministry. He was never alone in the presence of a female other than his wife. The anecdotal story is that he was once riding an elevator alone and it stopped at a floor, the doors opened, and a woman walked in. Dr. Graham, realizing that he would ride this elevator for several floors alone with this woman, immediately jumped out and took the stairs. Even a short, 30 second journey in an elevator with this female could've sidelined his ministry. Had she accused him of something, how could he have defended himself? For him, this practice was wise.

For many people, *The Billy Graham Rule* seems too extreme and impractical. In the workplace, especially, meetings and conferences and conversations are a must, and sometimes being alone with a member of the opposite sex is virtually unavoidable. However, you still need rules for your marriage. You and your spouse need a set of guidelines to protect both of you from walking down the destructive road of infidelity. If *The Billy Graham Rule* isn't realistic, then what is? What rules will help you safeguard your marriage?

To help you and your spouse think through what is best for your marriage, here are a few of our rules and how we implement them in our lives:

1 — We do not ride in the car or have a meal alone with someone of the opposite sex. If I (Kevin) have a meeting across town, and a coworker of the opposite sex is in that meeting, we drive separately. Or we include a third person in that meeting. If someone of the opposite sex really wants to meet me (Kevin) for a meal, I invite Katie. We'd rather pay a babysitter the $30 or $40 than risk the appearance of something inappropriate or open the door to a dangerous path.

2 — We have no secrets. NONE. Surprises are fine. Secrets are not. I (Kevin) never tell a coworker or friend something I would not also tell Katie. I (Katie) never share with a friend something I would hide from Kevin. The only exception to this is if one of us happened to be meeting with a marriage counselor for help in our marriage.

3 — We share passwords, phones, and emails with one another. We have complete freedom to check one another's phones, read texts, emails, and see who the other has called. We rarely do so (we don't have time or much interest), but we know we have the freedom to look at one another's communications anytime we desire.

4 — Our finances are completely combined. This has been challenging, at times, when I (Kevin) have wanted to surprise Katie with a gift. I've actually had a friend purchase the gift and then repay them after it was given. Other than those (rare) times we are surprising one another, we always know what the other has spent.

5 — We never criticize our spouse to a member of the opposite sex. And, honestly, we rarely ever do so to a member of the same sex. I (Katie) might say to a friend, in jest, something like, "Having to preach on Sundays makes Kevin the most boring guy in town on Saturday nights." When Katie was pregnant with our first child and working full time, we went out to eat virtually every night. I'm sure I (Kevin) probably said something like, "This year I've hidden Katie's Christmas present in the oven. I know she'll never find it there."

However, that's as far as it goes. We never seriously complain about one another to others. When this is done with coworkers or friends of the opposite sex, the door is opened to a special bond being formed with someone other than your spouse.

6 — We communicate A LOT. Throughout the day, by text and phone. If we don't know something about what's happening in the other's life, it's because we've just forgotten to mention it or we've been busy with life. We share a common calendar on our phones, and we generally know exactly what the other is doing at any given moment in the day.

7 — We travel together. We take at least one or two times a year to get away, just us, no kids. Most years, these are just quick trips to the beach or I (Katie) will tag along with Kevin to a conference he's attending. Some years we'll actually get to do a big trip together, typically an overseas experience. We've found these to be especially helpful for our marriage because 1) we both really enjoy traveling and 2) we actually get lots of time to talk without being interrupted. Our conversations are able to go beyond discussions about feeding the dog or making sure one of us is available to drive our son to football practice. We use these occasions to talk about our dreams, our desires, or areas in life where we are struggling... conversations similar to those we had when we were dating!

Far too many individuals have traveled down the dangerous

road of adultery, only to later find themselves full of regrets. What guardrails do you need to protect your marriage? As you and your spouse discuss these questions, begin developing your own list. Build a solid fence around your relationship. Do whatever it takes to keep your marriage safe.

QUESTIONS

1   What rules do you think we should live by in our marriage? Are there things I'm doing now that bother you? What changes should we make?

2   Is there anyone of the opposite sex that you're uncomfortable with me being around? Why? Are there appropriate boundaries we can set with this individual?

3   Am I on my phone or tablet too much? When would you like me to be disconnected from technology?

4   Do I ever speak about you to others in a way that makes you uncomfortable or embarrassed? Can you remember specific examples? Are there times I feel like I'm just joking, but it's offensive to you?

5   Do you know how I spend our money? If not, do you want to know? How can we be transparent with one another in the area of our finances?

6   We need to have at least one vacation a year that's just us, even if it's just an overnight getaway. How can we make that happen? (*Hint*: do we have enough credit card points banked so we can do this inexpensively?)

7   Let's make it a goal to talk for at least fifteen minutes a day without being interrupted. How can we make that happen?

8   Is there anything not mentioned yet that could help us affair-proof our marriage?

DO THE ROAR!

Managing www.ourhouse.biz

There is a scene in the movie, *Shrek*, where Shrek is at a birthday party with his three children. (Are they called "children" or is there another word used to signify the offspring of ogres?) The entire party is complete chaos. Pinocchio is performing a repetitive, annoying kids song, and Donkey is giving Shrek grief about not singing along. One of his children is squeezing a toy next to Shrek's ear, the incessant squeaking sending bolts of pain through Shrek's brain. Shrek retrieves the birthday cake from the baker, only to have Donkey lick the icing, putting a tongue-streak right through the middle of the decoration on the top.

Shrek's mother-in-law then accuses Shrek of licking the cake, since that's obviously what an ogre would do. His wife tasks him with guarding the cake while she gets candles. He turns his back for half a second and the three little pigs devour it. The children are crying, his wife is upset with him, and the room is full of noise and activity. The icing on this cake of chaos (pun intended) is a kid using his nasally voice to repeatedly demand that Shrek "do the roar." Apparently, the roar of an ogre is notoriously powerful, and this tiny malcontent won't be satisfied until Shrek gives him what he wants. As Shrek's world seems to be spinning out of control, the annoying voice of this kid barks over and over, "*Do the roar! Do the roar! Do the roar!*"

Shrek loses it. He does "the roar," and then begins a journey that would become the main plot of the movie. He wants a day off. One day free from his wife…his children… the chaos…everything. He just needs a break. To obtain this, he trades a day with Rumpelstiltskin, the evil antagonist who is after more than just one day of Shrek's life. Shrek reluctantly signs a contract with this man, despite his misgivings, simply because he needs one day of freedom from the busyness and chaos of his family life.

Does any of that sound familiar? Have you ever felt the same way?

As I (Kevin) write this chapter, I'm sitting in my car at 8 PM on a Monday evening. It's been a wild, whirlwind evening. I left work early and drove home to help Katie prepare for a family birthday party. She worked most of the afternoon getting food and decorations ready. Family members arrived at our house, and everyone had a great time. Except... our children seemed especially demanding. Our family dog continually attempted to steal food from the plates of our unsuspecting children. There was lots of noise, a huge mess in the kitchen after dinner, and it's a school night. Meaning, after all of the chaos of the evening, we still have homework to get finished, baths to take and give, pajamas to put on, children to get tucked in, and preparing for tomorrow. The evening just felt extremely chaotic, and I was very much aware that more chaos was coming. No one begged me to do the roar, but I think I would've happily obliged if I'd been asked.

At a certain point, I made my escape. I went into the garage and sat in the driver's seat of my car. I retrieved my laptop from my bag sitting in the passenger's seat. I began writing this chapter, for personal therapy more than the need to finish a book. At some point, Katie will notice I'm not in the house. Perhaps she already has. She's calling my name, going from room to room, needing help with baths, getting kids to bed, reading a book to our youngest two children, keeping the dog from mischief, or any number of other things I'd normally be doing this time of night. At some point she'll probably open the door to our garage and discover me sitting in my car, hot and sweaty, typing on my computer. "What in the world are you doing?" she'll ask.

"Looking up contact information on Rumpelstiltskin."

"What?!?"

"Never mind. I'll explain later."

Don't judge me. You've done the same thing at some point. Maybe you didn't escape to the hot garage, but I bet you've hidden in a closet or gone to the corner of your backyard. When caught, you claimed you were organizing hangers or pulling weeds. The truth is that you just needed fifteen minutes to yourself. Or maybe thirty. Or perhaps you considered trading that day of your life for a day of freedom. Just be careful signing those contracts. That Rumple is a scoundrel.

If you've ever felt this way, just know how much you're not alone. Running *www.ourhouse.biz* can be absolutely exhausting. If you have young children at home, then you can easily get worn down from the whining, the crying, the neediness of little voices and their constant requests. "Mommy, tie my shoe again. Daddy, I can't find my Legos. I'm hungry. I'm thirsty. I'm bored. I want you to play with me." It is so taxing and seems to just suck brain cells right out of your ears.

If you have older children, tweens, or young teenagers, then you probably feel like you're an Uber driver, taking passengers to and from school, sports practices, lessons, and friend's houses. You swore you'd never drive a minivan, but now you're loving the automatic doors. You push the button, the door slides open, and you just shove a kid or two out before heading to your next stop.

If you have older teenagers, then you're a nervous wreck and you're absolutely broke. When your oldest turned sixteen and passed their driver's test, you were elated. "Finally, I'm free," you thought. "I can pass this non-paying Uber gig off to my eldest." Then you received your auto insurance premium. Now you sit at home in the dark house because you've turned off all the lights to save on your energy bill. You're excited to now have some peace and quiet, but you really wish you had some money to take a trip, go out to eat, or to buy a couple of steaks to grill. You can't believe you're eating Ramen noodles again.

Each stage of raising children brings unique challenges and stresses, all of which will potentially cause problems in your marriage. Katie and I have felt at times that we are simply partners in this business we call "Our House," and all of our conversations revolve around effectively running this company.

Getting on the same page as partners in this business is critical. Communication, communication, and more communication is absolutely necessary. This week's exercise certainly isn't very romantic, but coordination and agreement in this area of your marriage will make a big difference in your relationship. In other words, agreement in the kitchen will make for better times in the bedroom.

QUESTIONS

1   How are we doing dividing the responsibilities of our life together? Do we know which of us handles car maintenance, cleaning the house, keeping up with kids' school needs, buying groceries, yard work, purchasing clothes for the kids, etc.?

2   Are we doing a good job coordinating our calendar? How can we do it better?

3   Are our children involved in too many extra-curricular activities? Do we need to place any limits on what they are doing?

4   Let's revisit the question from last week about having 15 minutes to talk without being interrupted. How can we schedule at least a brief time to meet each day? (For example, we have our daily "meeting" each day right after dinner. Once everyone has eaten, we send the kids away and we spend fifteen minutes talking about life.)

5   Is there any specific way we can improve the way our house operates?

6   Are we asking our children to do enough chores? What changes should we make?

7   Do we have healthy and appropriate limits on the use of technology in our home? Do our children both understand and follow these rules?

8   What are we doing to disciple our children? Are we creating an environment where they are learning to love God and others?

9   Are there any family traditions that are important to you or that you'd like to create?

10 Are there any other areas of *www.ourhouse.biz* that need improvement?

WEEK 6

THREE'S COMPANY

Putting God at the Center of Your Relationship

A tremendously wise individual once recorded a powerful truth that applies to marriage: *"Though one may be overpowered, two can defend themselves. A cord of three strands is not quickly broken"* (Ecclesiastes 4:12). This "third strand" of our marriage is Christ. From the genesis of our relationship, our goal has been to keep our marriage centered on him. Whenever our hearts have become disconnected, he has been faithful to rebuke our oversized egos and show us the way back to one another.

We've had fights in our marriage that have left me (Katie) so furious with Kevin that I was unwilling to forgive. In fact, I didn't even want to speak to him. I was angry and I was done. If there was to be reconciliation, he would need to make the first move.

Then, in a quiet moment, perhaps sitting in a chair in our bedroom and sulking, or while driving my car away from our house to somewhere, anywhere, I would hear a small whisper. This faint voice would ask me a few simple questions: "What part did you play in this fight? How could you have handled that differently? How many times has Kevin had to forgive you? How many times have I had to forgive you?"

Slowly and steadily, the hardness of my heart would begin to soften. This third strand of our marriage would do what he's done so well, so many times before — bring truth to my mind and give me clarity on my own sin and responsibility in our marriage.

I (Kevin) have had similar experiences. I'm keenly aware of my accountability to this third strand of our marriage. It's similar to the way we deal with our children when they fight with one another. We will not only give correction for things they do or say to cause the conflict, but also instruction on the need to forgive. Sometimes, if we want to really make the point and drive them a little crazy in the process, we say "Now, you need to give each other a hug as well." Their little bodies cringe as they stiffly hug one another and grumble, "I forgive you." Perhaps their hearts aren't ready to reconcile, but they know they must because of their accountability to us.

I've found the Lord doing the same thing with me. As I sit to read my Bible and pray, I'll hear that still, small voice say, "You need to forgive" or "Have you considered your role in this fight?" or "Let's talk about how you can be a more loving husband." My love for God has increased my love for Katie. Katie's devotion to the Lord has made her more devoted to me. Putting God at the center of our marriage is a daily decision, but one that makes our relationship immeasurably better.

This third strand has given us the ability to show grace, the willingness to offer forgiveness, and the strength to fulfill the vows we made to each other. This third strand has been the foundation of our marriage and the key to its growth and health. As a twosome, our marriage likely would've failed years ago. As a trio, we've managed to navigate the trials, work through the rough patches, and celebrate the highs together. We've found a joy that otherwise we wouldn't have known. It's given us a center, a grounding, and a purpose in our lives. While there have been many struggles, we have always been able to return to this saving relationship we have found through Jesus Christ.

If you're reading this book and have never considered this aspect of your life and your marriage, this may just be a major turning point for you and your spouse. Think about the big picture of your marriage. Imagine the years beyond the fight you had last night or the frustrations you're having right now with your spouse. Consider the next year, decade, and several decades of your life. Better yet, consider your life one hundred years from now. What is your goal? What is the real purpose of your life? Are we really just supposed to live as long as we can, get as much as we can, and hope we have some fun along the way? Is life really nothing more than, "Eat, drink, and be merry, for tomorrow we die?"

Or, is there a greater purpose for your life? And for your

spouse? And your marriage? Has God placed you here on this earth for something more than just a mediocre kind of existence? In the big scheme of life, does God have some great plan for you and your marriage?

In John 10:10, Jesus said, "*I have come that they might have life, and have it abundantly.*" Jesus came and died to give us access to God and eternal life. Outside of Christ, you can have no spiritual life. You are dead and without hope. In Christ, however, there is the promise of eternal and abundant life. This doesn't mean you always get exactly what you want in life, but it does mean that a life centered on Jesus brings a joy and fulfillment otherwise unavailable to us.

Moreover, Jesus came that your marriage might be full of life. The last thing God desires is for you to be miserable in your current relationship. Your marriage is designed for joy and happiness. You and your spouse have access to abundance in your marriage.

Right now, if your marriage is really struggling, perhaps God is the missing ingredient. There is no third strand of your marriage. Either you or your spouse aren't followers of Christ, or you are but God isn't at the center of your marriage. The children, sports, your job, hobbies, money, or something else is central in your marriage, but Jesus isn't.

Is this your turning point? Perhaps the way to reignite joy in your marriage is to make it a trio. Invite God to be the third and most important strand of your relationship.

If this is something you haven't done, we strongly encourage you to end these exercises by praying together and committing yourselves and your marriage to God. When you do, God will be faithful to not only be the glue of your relationship, but to bring your marriage great abundance as well.

QUESTIONS

1   Are we making worship / church attendance the priority it needs to be?

2   What can I do to help you find time to read your Bible and spend some quality moments with God each day?

3   Are there ways we can serve together?

4   How can I be praying for you, our marriage, and our family?

5   How can I help you cultivate godly friendships? Do you have someone in your life who is encouraging you and holding you accountable?

6   Are we sharing our faith with others: our neighbors, coworkers, or those we know socially? How can we do a better job with this?

7   What would you like your spiritual life to look like 10 years from now? Is there anything I can do to help you get there?

8   Are we leaving the kind of legacy we want to leave? How can we be more intentional in doing this?

9   Imagine our lives as "old people" sitting in rocking chairs on a porch somewhere. What are the top two or three things you want people to say about us and our marriage? What do we need to do now for these things to be said about us then?

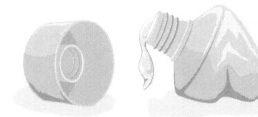

CONCLUSION

We'd completed the book and passed it to an editor when we heard the news: another couple divorcing after years of marriage. They are both successful in their careers, have children together, are financially well-to-do, have many friends, traveled together often, and seemed to have a great marriage.

It wasn't.

Evidently, things really weren't good between these two. They weren't happy. In fact, with all of the expenses and troubles of their divorce (moving, legal fees, setting up new accounts with utility companies, changing bank accounts, scheduling holiday visits... the list goes on for pages) we assume that the marriage was downright miserable. And, perhaps, had been that way for years.

WHY TOOTHPASTE MATTERS

We know it didn't begin that way. They were, at one time, genuinely happy and very much in love. They dated, married, purchased a home together, had children, joined a church, went on vacations, and celebrated holidays with each other's families. They were — as the Bible describes a married couple — *one*. Now, however, that's no longer the case. Their relationship became so strained that two who had become one went back to being two.

Sadly, their story isn't unique. It happens all the time. Too many marriages begin with great hope and promise, but end with pain and heartbreak.

Sure, marriage is challenging. We've covered this truth in the book. However, your spouse can and should be the greatest human blessing of your life. You have a teammate, a friend, a lover, a travel companion, and a partner in everything you face. You get to do life with this individual. You get to celebrate the joys you experience together and lean on one another during difficult days. We hope and pray that every couple who reads these words will view their marriage as this great blessing. We pray that your marriage will not just be good, but wonderfully great.

This is the end of the book, but not the end of your need to continually work on your marriage. Tend to that garden. Prioritize your marriage. Strive for a relationship that is strong and healthy. Then, when the day comes that you and your spouse are old and gray, sitting in rocking chairs on a front porch somewhere and holding hands, you'll be able to smile at one another and say, "Thank God we finally started buying separate tubes of toothpaste."

CONCLUSION

WHY TOOTHPASTE MATTERS

ENDNOTES

1   "In Your Eyes," written and performed by Peter Gabriel for his solo album, "So." Produced by Peter Gabriel, Bill Laswell and Daniel Lanois. 1986.

2   "You're The Inspiration," Written by Peter Cetera and David Foster for the group, Chicago, and released on their album Chicago 17. Produced by David Foster. 1984.

3   "The Glory of Love," written by Peter Cetera, David Foster, and Diane Nini. 1986.

4   "Hard to Say I"m Sorry" Written by Peter Cetera and David Foster for the group, Chicago, and released on their album Chicago 16. Produced by David Foster. 1982.

ABOUT THE AUTHORS

Kevin and Katie live in Macon, Georgia with their four kids and crazy Golden Doodle. They've been happily (and sometimes slightly less than happily) married since 2005. After spending a year living and working together in Rome, Italy, Kevin was called to serve as the lead pastor of Northway Church, where he has served since 2007. Katie runs a faith, family, and lifestyle blog at www.thejoyfullyimperfect.com. They have a heart for ministry, adoption, travel, tunes by Van Morrison, and separate tubes of toothpaste or any other practical life hacks that make their marriage stronger.

Made in the USA
Columbia, SC
07 January 2020

86459027R10088

Made in the USA
Las Vegas, NV
16 October 2021

32463077R00106